After 50
It's Up to Us

*Developing the Skills
And Agility We'll Need*

George H. Schofield, Ph.D.

Foreword by Richard Nelson Bolles,
author of *What Color Is Your Parachute?*

TheClarityGroup

The Clarity Group, Inc.
P O Box 470966, San Francisco, CA 94147-0966
(415) 693 9719 and (415) 720 2601
www.clarity-group.com • www.georgeschofield.com

Book and cover design by Michael Brechner / Cypress House
Cover illustration by John S. Dykes / Getty Images

Publisher's Cataloging-in-Publication Data

Schofield, George H.
  After fifty it's up to us : developing the skills and agility we'll need /
George H. Schofield. -- 1st ed. -- San Francisco : Clarity Group,
2007.
    p. ; cm.
  ISBN-13: 978-0-9790382-4-2 (pbk.)
  ISBN-10: 0-9790382-4-3 (pbk.)
1. Older people--Life skills guides. 2. Aging--Psychological
aspects. 3. Retirement--Planning. 4. Self-management
(Psychology) I. Title.
  HQ1061 .S36 2007   2007922078
  646.7/9--dc22 0703

Printed in the USA
9 8 7 6 5 4 3 2

Permissions

Quotations on pp. 2 and 132 reprinted with the permission of Simon & Schuster Adult Publishing Group from *The Fountain of Age,* copyright © 1993 by Betty Friedan.

Poem on pp. 19–20 reprinted by permission of author Peggy Lynn Hill.

Quotations on pp. 42 and 127 reprinted by permission of *Harvard Business Review* from "It's Time to Retire Retirement" by Ken Dychtwald, Tamara Erickson, and Bob Morison, March 2004. Copyright © 2004 by the Harvard Business School Publishing Corp. All rights reserved.

Quotation on p. 42 from *The Coming Generational Storm* by Laurence J. Kotlikoff and Scott Burns reprinted by permission of The MIT Press, copyright © 2004.

Quotations on pp. 27 and 47 from *Successful Aging* reprinted by permission of Creative Management, Inc. Copyright 1998 by John Wallis Rowe, M.D. and Robert L. Kahn, Ph.D.

Excerpt on p. 48 from "The Cyber Future: 93 Ways Our Lives Will Change by the Year 2025" by Edward Cornish is used with permission from the World Future Society, 7910 Woodmont Ave., Suite 450, Bethesda, MD 20814. Tel: 301/656-8274; Fax: 301/951-0394; www.wfs.org.

Quotation on p. 49 from "Retire Early? Think Again," article by Jane Bryant Quinn, *Newsweek,* July 21, 2003, copyright © 2003 by the Washington Post Company.

Quotation on p. 65 from *The Third Age: Six Principles for Personal Growth and Renewal After Forty* by William A. Sadler, Ph.D. reprinted by permission of The Perseus Books Group, copyright © 2000.

Quotation on p.76 from *Will the Circle Be Unbroken?* reprinted with the permission of The New Press. Copyright © 2001 by Studs Terkel.

Quotation on p. 77 reprinted with the permission of Simon & Schuster Adult Publishing Group from *Awaken the Giant Within* by Anthony Robbins. Copyright ©1991 by Anthony Robbins.

Dedication

For Linda de Mello, my wife and partner, with deep appreciation for her constant and unconditional support as I pursued my own interests, skills, and agility after fifty.

Acknowledgments

I want to acknowledge the very important people who have deliberately or unwittingly pushed my awareness and abilities far beyond where they otherwise would have been: Linda de Mello, Argentine Craig, Neil Weinberg, Barbara Snider, Steve Carnevale, Harry Dawson, Todd and Danielle Schofield, Kevin and Jennifer Schofield, and Andrew Schofield and Janie Kint.

Thanks for support and inspiration of a thousand kinds: Steve Carnevale and Kelly Gorman, Blue Oak, Janis MacKenzie, Cate Cummings, Mary Laxague, Peggy Hill, Sam Khoury, Dick Bolles, Kathryn Johnson, Margaret Speaker Yuan, Alan Abeles, John Trauth, Cynthia Frank, and Howard and Judy Chermak.

Contents

Foreword

The author of this book, my friend George Schofield, is a man on a quest.

This is a decade when the first of baby boomers are turning fifty, a trickle that will soon turn into a floodtide. George—who is himself past fifty—is searching for tools that will help all those who are facing this milestone. He quotes some of the true pioneers in this research: Ken Dychtwald, William Bridges, Po Bronson, Studs Terkel, William Sadler, John Rowe and Robert Kahn, and Betty Friedan. He quotes the latter approvingly, where she speaks of this time of life as a stage "where there are no prescribed role models to follow, no guideposts, no rigid rules or visible rewards...."

George wants to find role models and guideposts. Toward this end, he is conducting endless interviews with those he calls modern-day "After-fifty Pioneers," to see if he can discern from their stories the tools that he, and the others, now need. He asked them such questions as "major fear about aging after fifty," and "major daily struggle after fifty," and "major surprise about life after fifty."

The interviews continue (you can go to his website, www.georgeschofield.com, and contribute your own story). But, with enough interviews under his belt, George has made this book at least his interim report.

"After-fifty," he has concluded, is a time best described as an "open life space," in which we need a greater vocabulary. His contribution toward that vocabulary is words that dominate the pages of this book: "skills" and "agility" and "the Wall" and "paradox" and "identity anchors" and "strong convoys" vs. "weak convoys." He identifies the Four Most Essential Abilities, the Three Truths, and the 10 Key Realities After Fifty.

People like to talk about making plans—for retirement, or whatever. George is wiser. He knows the truth that Martin Luther King Jr. once wrote about, the truth that the genius of life involves learning how to deal with interruptions—interruptions to our expectations, to our dreams, and to our plans. And so, for everyone searching not for planning but for tools to deal with interruptions after fifty, this book should prove enlightening, helpful, and inspiring.

— Richard Nelson Bolles, author,
   What Color Is Your Parachute?

Begin here at the beginning. By itself, reading won't be enough. Moving straight into action without reading won't work either.

Developing the Skills and Agility We'll Need for the Rest of Our Lives

On the Unfolding Road After Fifty

If you'd like to connect with experience, tenacity, and inspiration, try interviewing a wide variety of individuals between the ages of fifty and ninety-seven. In doing the research for this book I did just that. It was my privilege to hear the honest life stories and expectations of people pioneering life after fifty for themselves. Their wisdom is the heart of this book.

What inspired me was the participants' consistent sense of excitement about the opportunity to make the next part of their lives rich and rewarding. Their predictable concerns about aging and financial security in later life were more than offset by the realization that, after fifty, we bring so much more to the table than ever before: the sum of our experience, our depth of understanding, our self-confidence and determination, our appreciation of how transient and therefore how precious life is—in short, our hard-won accumulated wisdom. We earned this, and we not only deserve to create exciting, fulfilling lives after fifty, but we owe it to ourselves to make the very best of the endless possibilities awaiting us.

The question we face is much bigger than when or whether we retire. We have to figure out what we want our lives to be like, and remember that no matter what we select it won't be permanent. It will have to change and adapt as we grow older, and so will we. The "there" our parents planned to arrive at won't exist for us.

There are lots of examples of success to follow, and too many choices, too much change, and too many unknowns for us to assume we can always know in advance what we'll have to be good at as our lives unfold from here. Even with great planning, we'll need to be more agile than ever. We'll have to invent our lives and aging for ourselves, probably more than once. We don't yet know what abilities we could need later. Control is much easier than exercising our influence intelligently, but we have only so much control of our unfolding road. Realistically, we'll need to be flexible, adapt on a daily basis, pay close attention, and develop the right skills and agility.

Meet Some Truths
For After-fifty Pioneers

The problem is, first of all, how to break through the cocoon of our illusory youth and risk a new stage in life, where there are no prescribed role models to follow, no guideposts, no rigid rules or visible rewards, to step out into the true existential unknown of these new years of life now open to us, and to find our terms for living it.

Betty Friedan, *The Fountain of Age*

After fifty can be a time of opportunity and shift. At some point most of us experience:

- emancipation by the departure of grown children;
- a shift in the importance and place of work in our lives and sense of ourselves;
- awakening of new or resurgent interests together with some loss of interest in activities we've pursued for years;

- evaporation of roles we've fulfilled dutifully for decades;
- accomplishment or abandonment of long-held goals;
- death of our parents, death of peers or heroes, and even the death of some of our previous opponents and enemies
- release from some of the financial responsibility for others we carried for many years;
- increase in financial pressure with the sense that we're running out of time to provide for ourselves in the long term.

With these opportunities and shifts comes taking unprecedented responsibility for ourselves. The research for this book disclosed that many of us will immediately refill with busyness the open life space created by some of these shifts. The courageous ones among us will live with that newly opened space for a while. All the individuals I interviewed, who sat awhile with the open space, inevitably noticed, often with some discomfort, being faced with three truths for after-fifty pioneers:

Truth #1

We have the first real opportunity in years to focus on ourselves, and there's no one else to hold accountable if we're not doing it successfully or at all.

By the time we reach our early fifties, most of us have devoted our lives to fulfilling a variety of roles: son, daughter, friend, worker, professional, parent, homeowner, neighbor, volunteer. We don't want to abandon these now so much as we want to be real about making choices for our future that we took for granted earlier in our busy lives. Aging will happen anyway. Should we take care of our health? Absolutely. Manage our finances well? Of course. Should we develop and enjoy stimulating interests? Certainly. Will life go totally according to plan? Probably not—it seldom has before. We simply want to focus on our choices and responsibilities each day in a more conscious way than we ever have before. We want to pioneer for ourselves, not live someone else's highly marketed vision of what we should do, who we should be, and what we should buy.

In our fifties, many of us experience the need to be more deliberate and conscious about our planning: financial condition, physical health, intentions, activities and interests, and whom we choose to spend our time with. Along with that new emphasis on planning come our forays into a huge number of people and companies wanting to provide us all the specialized planning services we can imagine: financial planning, healthcare planning, residential planning, social planning, activity planning, and plans for parts of our future lives we hadn't even imagined, much less thought we'd need to plan.

Most of us, hopefully, are doing the appropriate kinds of financial, legal, and health planning. We're using the services of the many fine planners whose expertise we need to anticipate our future financial and health needs.

Those among us who do all the right planning will eventually notice, often with some discomfort and a sense of familiarity, that they're faced with the second of the three truths for after-fifty pioneers:

Truth #2

Solid planning is imperative, and life is often what happens while we're making other plans.

Despite our best efforts at planning and getting it all organized, the unexpected arises, derailing our carefully crafted plans. We'll need to be great at flexibility, being able to work effectively with what is, sometimes accepting it and sometimes changing it.

In our fifties, many of us find ourselves at the peak of our game so far, our abilities honed and our experience stacked in accessible and usable form. We've achieved a certain amount of success and have even come to grips with some of our limitations. If we're paying attention, we have a heightened awareness of what's really going on with us.

With this awareness can come the realization that in our dramatically changing world, our movement through our fifties and beyond will call our accumulated skills into question. The courageous among us will see and admit to the third of the three truths for after-fifty pioneers:

Truth #3

We have developed abilities and approaches to life that have made us reasonably successful by age fifty, but those might not be what make us successful far beyond fifty. In fact, the abilities and approaches we've relied on the most before fifty could work against us later.

We've assumed roles, built lives with many forms of accomplishment, gotten good at what it took to succeed, and out of that mix have created identities and ways of being in the world. Nonetheless, I know from the many interviews I conducted for this book that the strengths we developed before fifty might not necessarily be the strengths that serve us best later in life.

We All Arrive at After Fifty Carrying Our Biographies and Expertise

By the time we pass fifty we've accumulated a lot of experience, several biographic segments, and a lot of expertise that comes from living our biographies one day at a time. In the midst of our daily efforts and busyness, it's easy to lose track of what we're really good at and what serves us well. Sometimes we need to stop for a little while and do some reflection on (1) our different biographic chapters; and (2) the expertise we developed in each of them. Chapters can be chronological;

they can also be thematic, capturing themes that repeat periodically in our lives.

Our biographies are diverse. Yours is unique to you even if it shares some characteristics with others'. Here's an analysis I did of my own life's learning through my chapters:

Biographic Chapter

I became a single parent when my sons were under eight, certainly not what I planned. This was when the world still thought women couldn't run businesses and men couldn't parent alone. I learned behaviors and identities associated with both male and female parents. By the time my sons were in their late teens, they'd given me a full understanding of the difference between control and influence. I learned to show up every day and be as able as I could with what was in front of me. I didn't remarry until long after the boys were out on their own.

Expertise

Expertise in finding the next task to accomplish or obstacle to outwit. Expertise in balancing control and influence in any given situation.

Expertise in a combination of: (1) ability to set myself aside and listen deeply; (2) genuine interest in what the person has to say; and (3) fascination with others' interests that I know little or nothing about.

Expertise in anticipating, but not inserting myself into, what I could see flowing into my son's lives—positive or negative.

A BA in Business, an MA in Counseling, an MA in Adult Learning, and a Ph.D. in Human and Organizational Development.

Expertise in research, writing, and speaking on the wide range of topics that interest me.

Expertise in human development, the knowledge of how we grow and adapt, or fail to, over our life spans. The price of this is the stress involved when a client isn't yet ready to do the work, but is obviously beginning to suffer.

Expertise in organizational development, knowing how organizations grow and adapt, or fail to, over their life spans.

Expertise in seeking new ideas and possibilities, the price of which can be failure to see and appreciate what I already know.

Biographic Chapter

A long-standing reputation for work with career management and job-search clients. Individuals and corporations both have career paths with often-shared flex points, though we usually don't think of it that way. I was cited in the "Finding Help: A Sampler" appendix of Richard Bolles's groundbreaking What Color Is Your Parachute?

Expertise

Expertise in applied research: What's really going on here; what's it costing us not to change; what are our options; which are the best ones; and how do we implement them?

Expertise in understanding and working with individuals and couples who've moved past the job-search into the far more demanding and creative search for the right fit and opportunities for work in middle and later adulthood.

Biographic Chapter

I earned my stripes over thirty-five years of full-time employment in the corporate world, from vice president at the Bank of America, to senior regional leader in a multinational consulting company, to having my own company specializing in research-based business solutions.

Expertise

Expertise in the realities of the corporate world of work and change at individual, team, and organizational levels.

Expertise in moving on from common questions to those whose answers yield effective and integrative solutions.

When I did this exercise, I asked, "If I'm such an expert, shouldn't I be excused from having to do this investigation of my unfolding road after fifty?" No! There's no testing out of life, even for an expert in something.

I felt led into doing the research for this book, and not just for my own learning and development. My professional and academic backgrounds gave me an intense interest in:

- getting much clearer on the questions I need to ask myself about living a skillful, agile life after fifty, the quality of the answers depending on the quality of the questions;

- the widespread, similar searching I could see my after-fifty friends, neighbors, and colleagues doing to identify the right questions and workable answers for themselves.

Now is the time to start a notebook, which you'll be using repeatedly as you read on. Begin by listing your expertise from your own biography. You can use the same two-column format I used. You can group your chapters by stages of your life, roles you've played, themes that have run through your biography, or any other form of grouping that works for you. When you're done, discuss what you've written with someone you trust who is:

1. interested in you and your development;

2. able to separate his or her sense of personal okay-ness from what you've written;

3. likely to be insightful about you, what has served you well in the past, and what you might need to develop in the future.

My research started out just for me, but it turned out to be this book for all of us approaching or past fifty. In the beginning, I had little interest in *aging* or *elderly* per se. Information on avoiding aging in one way or another is plastered all over the advertising we see. There's plenty of information on aging and elderly, and a mountain of literature on financial planning, gerontology, keeping busy and active, health and healthcare planning, next place or career, retirement, travel, and the coming generational conflict over life space, resources, and power.

My approach began with an attitude of "I don't know what I don't know." After doing enough interviews to confirm my direction and suspicions, I was struck by how little practical, example-based information there is out there on "after fifty it's up to us" and on skills and agility, so I decided to continue the research and see if a helpful book might emerge.

I began questioning my colleagues, my wife, and my closest friends. Almost everyone's first response involved "the importance of planning." The second response was "Of course, planning can only take you so far." This echoed my corporate consulting work, in which people say, as they hand me the organization chart, "Of course, this isn't the way things really work around here."

I found I wasn't alone in my search for answers in a changing world; lots of people around me were asking: "Who do I want to be when I reach age seventy or eighty or ninety?" "How do I learn to operate in the world as aging becomes a greater part of my life, even though I feel nowhere close to old now?" "What will I have to be good at? Will it be the same as in the past?" "Do I want more of the same, or do I want something really different?" "I'm overwhelmed with the growing amount to read and learn. How do I choose where to devote my attention?"

Eventually, every research participant got around to talking about the importance of *skills* and *agility*.

The network of friends and research participants—almost all of whom decided to actively help recruit others—grew. Participants, ranging from fifty to ninety-seven years of age, were from all over the US and from many walks of life. Each completed a research survey that asked for both quantitative and qualitative data. Each sat with me and talked—some would call it an interview—for between ninety and 120 minutes. I recorded the conversations.

I was after a substantial number of diverse participants who would provide representative insights about skills, agility, and experiential knowledge that I knew lived in their stories and expectations. Knowing how very individual our lives are—though we share aspects in common—I was after the questions that provoke answers that come closest to wisdom.

In the end, all the participants were everyday people who were enormously generous with their time. They didn't have extraordinary education or wealth or expertise in human development. They were all thoughtful in their individual ways, and all interested in pushing their own envelopes of abilities and possibilities.

As an experienced interviewer and human development expert, I thought I had reasonable expectations about what people would have to say. I wasn't prepared for their outpouring of energy, curiosity, reflection, candidness, vulnerability, and pioneering that our working together produced.

This is a practical, hands-on book about skills and agility, and the difference they can make in the quality of our lives from fifty on. You'll read about the importance of planning, and even more about the capacity to live life well as it inevitably goes not quite according to plan. You're going to meet some very interesting people.

I'm hoping to inspire reflective, informed conversation within and between readers now that would otherwise wait until a later time, when learning and adaptability might be much harder to master. I'm hoping to bring new vocabulary to the conversations we'll need to have, for which there's not yet enough new language and few proven models of skills and agility after fifty.

Finally, this is a book that combines:

1. pioneering ideas about skills and agility and the key abilities needed after fifty;

2. real stories of people from their fifties into their eighties;

3. the opportunity for you to evaluate and learn from their stories;

4. the opportunity for you to see, work with, and discuss your own skill and agility and the responsibilities and choices that accompany them.

I guaranteed anonymity to my research participants and have honored that. The composite people you'll meet in this book all tell their truth. They're courageous in their willingness to share their stories, and are committed to using their skills and agility. It's my fond hope that from understanding their stories, we can improve the quality of our individual and collective pioneering.

An Invitation To Join in the Skills and Agility Conversation

A lot of people felt passion for my research. This book is a way to share the results and join in a longer, larger dialog that can benefit all of us at fifty and beyond. Please write to me; go to my website, www.georgeschofield.com. Tell me something new from your experience that will add to the conversation. For example:

- your own stories of skills and agility beyond fifty;
- what you're discovering that you need to honor yet leave behind beyond fifty;
- the best examples of your own skills and agility beyond fifty;
- what has surprised you the most about your learning beyond fifty;
- your self-observations that would make a great addition to the next edition of *After Fifty It's Up To Us*.

My thanks to all the research participants and readers of this book for being such great companions as we pioneer the rest of our lives together. Your wisdom and experience can inform and help all of us.

George H. Schofield
San Francisco, California
January 2007

The Wall is our friend.
It may shake us up as it gets our attention,
but real friendship and value are seldom free.

Chapter 1

Running Into The Wall Again

Is this book for you? Here's a quick test:

- Are you approaching or past fifty?
- Are you willing to invest a reasonable amount of time and energy in your future?
- Will the rest of your life go according to plan?
- Do you have all the abilities and awareness on which you can build reliable skills and agility for use in a rapidly changing world after fifty?

If your answers are yes, yes, no, and no, then this book is for you.

I didn't plan to tell my own story in this book; the stories of others seemed much more intriguing. Yet every person I interviewed asked how I'd become interested in the topic. When I answered, they all said, "Your story needs to be the first chapter!" It wasn't just about me, but my life was the starting point. I observed for years that I needed to practice in my own career what I taught people to do in theirs. I decided to honor that same commitment to integrity in writing the first chapter of *After Fifty It's Up To Us*. I knew mine was called "my life" for a good reason, so, as I began the interviews, I started telling them, "It's called *your life* for a reason." We all that agreed this ownership was a starting place.

I grew up in a typical American city in the 1940s and '50s, graduating from high school in 1962, slightly ahead of the baby boomers. I lived a life common to many young people in that era. Our family drove Chevrolets, Dodges, and Mercurys. We attended church, in our case Protestant.

My parents' developmental experiences, like most parents of the era, included the Great Depression and World War II. Not surprisingly, they had great faith in institutions and a huge need for structure and order. My parents were honorable and deeply human in their own ways. While I might not wish some of my early experiences for my children, if I hadn't had the parents and the childhood I had, I couldn't be who I am today.

My parents impressed upon me the same great truths that many of my peers, during our interviews, said their parents had told them:

- You can tell us anything.
- Climb the ladder of success.
- Wisdom comes with age and experience.
- The keys to success are perseverance and hard work.
- Take care of your employer well and he/they/it will take care of you.
- Do as I say, not as I do.
- Boys will be boys.
- Know your place.
- Nice boys don't eat with their hands.
- Save some money; you never know when you'll need it.
- The communists are out to get us.
- Wear clean underwear when you go to the doctor.

Dated as some of these sound today, they were central to how my parents thought of themselves and everything worthwhile in our lives. They couldn't have known that many of their great truths would turn out not to be true for my generation.

While I was in high school and still living at home, I discerned that there was going to be a large gap between my generation/world and my parents'. I understood that this had been true between my parents and their parents; the differences showed when the generations were together and unguarded. But I couldn't figure out what it all meant for me and my future.

So I launched into the '60s and '70s with my 1950s skills and values. Life did the rest. I found myself pursuing a number of tracks, most successfully, and found myself periodically lost and without my accustomed bearings. Along the way I did what many of my peers did: went to college, got married, had children, bought a house, developed a career, got divorced, and raised children as a single parent. I was far more liberal than my parents, though much less liberal than many. Until my father died at age eighty-four he would regularly say to me, "How did you get to be so liberal? Where did I go wrong?" I developed interests and activities, kept some, dropped others, and along the way, while I wasn't looking, I got older and developed a set of values appropriate to me and my life.

One of the things I most admire about my former brother-in-law, Mike, a retired automotive executive, is that he worked for the same company, doing variations of the same work, for thirty years. If it was in his character, it certainly wasn't in mine. The only thing I did thirty years running was devote myself to being a good parent.

Periodically, I would collide with The Wall. It happened before I got my divorce. It happened when I went to graduate school for the first time, and again when I earned my later-in-life Ph.D., and yet again when my pubescent sons drilled into me their wisdom about the difference between control and influence. It happened before each small and large career change. It happened when the bank I worked for broke the postwar contract for trust and mutual service between company and staff. It happened when I tried to save my mother's life and failed.

The Wall has played an important role in my life. It's never harmed me, though it's had to get emphatic to get my attention from time to time. It always knows before I do, and consistently gives me what psychologist Chuck Maurer taught me was my "blinding glimpse of the obvious." Of course, I had to be willing to pay attention for The Wall to be able to help me. While I've grown attached to my wall, not everyone has need of a wall and its capacity for temporary drama, attention getting, and promotion of learning. Still, it's possible that more people could occasionally use a wall.

In 2002 I met up with my old friend The Wall again. This collision felt particularly dramatic because I was fifty-eight and didn't fancy feeling surprised and without my usual sense of bearings at that age. I imagined I should have it all together and never find myself lost or in need of The Wall again. After all, fifty-eight!

I didn't see The Wall until I felt the impact. I had vaguely sensed it moving toward me while I was moving toward it, but, being someone who prefers the hope end of the continuum to the fear end, I hadn't really looked up. Fifty-eight doesn't sound so old until you're there, still thinking of yourself as thirty-five. I no longer knew all the popular music. I clung to "You're welcome" in a world that had converted to "No problem" while I wasn't looking. I couldn't begin to keep up with everything I wanted to read.

My wall is massive, and able to move fast with great agility. It has the word "paradox" spray-painted just above my reach. We're old colleagues, this wall and I, having collided many times before. My role has been to focus single-mindedly on whatever I'm working on at the time. The Wall's role has been to place itself in my path at the very moments I'm available to feel the impact and really pay attention to the essential lessons. Of the two of us, The Wall has displayed greater patience, finesse, timing, affection, and wisdom.

The word "Paradox" on The Wall used to be a puzzler. Not anymore. What does it mean for me and the people I interviewed?

Examples

- The freedom and the responsibility of independence;

- The heavy burdens and the huge gifts of parenthood;

- The assurance in religious commitment, and the lack of proof;

- Attachment to permanence, and the inevitability of loss;

- The loss of identity that can come with aging or retirement, and the great possibilities that re-crafting the self can offer if the loss is embraced;

- Being in the Zen-like space midway between non-attachment and total obsession.

This time, a large mirror hung on the wall. Looking back at me from its depths were my father's and mother's eyes, and a fifty-eight-year-old facial expression all my own. The expression was clear: "The developmental work you do now will affect the quality of your life and aging as surely as the nurturing a child receives affects the quality of its adulthood. Remember the paradox. Some important pieces of how you've crafted who you are and how you've operated successfully until now will no longer be effective; instead, they'll get in your way as your fifties turn into your sixties and beyond."

How do you thank a graffiti-sprayed wall and a mirror for their gifts of insight and compassion, difficult as they may be to handle? The answer: cherish the gifts and pass them on.

Here's a piece of a poem by Peggy Hill, whom I regard as a great poet.

Here we are
Trailing the patched cloth of our lives
Finely textured, worn with good use and familiar
But not always the stuff of sails

Giving it all a watchful whirl
Upon the strange green sea that stretches out before us

Relying on the sure hands we've watched
Knot the ropes beside us for decades
And two or three foreign navigators enlisted
For a time, this time, perhaps not more

We are free to write as quickly as we please
These new sea stories
In most any language that conveys the clearest meaning
Knowing between the holding fast and letting go
There will always be a place
Where the sail snaps taut and sure
Catching fresh breezes that will carry us between
Our certainties and our dreams

The Wall knew my dilemma before I knew it. Part one of my difficulty was clear: I was no longer grounded in what had been solid a few weeks before, yet nothing was wrong and there was nothing to solve. I was apparently right on schedule. Increased awareness and ability after fifty could be mine if I could do the learning without resorting to a problem/solution model.

In the past there had always been another goal. A long-time problem solver, I'd always sought problems for the gifts of their resolution. Now I had changed. Looking at self-help books, I found I didn't need more financial planning, want to "reinvent" myself for another round of career (especially when it meant starting all over again rather than bringing the most useful forward to add to what was to come), didn't need to work with my wife on our marriage or communication, didn't need to find another way to prove myself, and wasn't ready to sacrifice the rich diversity of our life to live primarily in a community of people in my own age, financial, educational, and special-interest groups.

It was scary. I had accomplished most of the things I'd set out to do. Many of the important roles I relied on for my identity and satisfaction—spouse, parent, professional, business owner—were no longer dominant in my sense of myself. Work and job titles validated me much less than they had. I hadn't given permission for most of these changes to occur.

What disturbed me most was having lots of questions and no answers, but knowing that the search for answers would be about building skill and agility, not solutions and change. I didn't want an upgraded future that looked like just another round of goals and steps, problems to solve, and challenges to overcome. I didn't want a plan that looked like an extension of my past. I'd been there. I wasn't nearly ready to "retire." Life after fifty needed to bring the best from earlier years and introduce a newness I couldn't yet define. And the right combination would probably continue to change for a long time to come.

Part two of my dilemma was less clear: could I learn to live with a changing balance of enough planning and adaptability (which I later came to call skills and agility) to steer an intelligent course between shorelines that were no longer stable?

I was busy in daily tasks, yet these subjects needed some high-quality time. To get it, I decided to run away from home. It was time to do the work of paying attention. My wife rented a condo for me in the Coachella Valley of Southern California. I drove down from San Francisco and stayed a week, alone and uninterrupted. What I discovered when I was willing to really engage was that I wasn't alone on this journey *and* I was again going to have to begin from the position of "I don't know what I don't know," rather than from my preferred position of "I know what I don't know, so let's go solve it."

My wife and I had agreed that toward the end of my sojourn she would fly down for a weekend, and we would then drive home together. By the time she arrived I'd had several days to reflect. I had covered the walls of the condo with sheets of paper, written and organized and written on some more at all hours as the spirit moved me. When she got there I gave her a guided tour, complete with visual aids, of what was going on with me and where this could be taking me.

Here are the highlights:

- Acknowledging that I'd done most of the things on the accomplishment list I was handed as a little boy, the list to which I added something new as soon as something else was checked off. This completion can be disorienting in a land where challenges and accomplishment are the stuff of life.

- A hatred of the boxes I had created, living in appropriate roles for my entire life. I had created professional and personal opportunities to match my personality and needs as I went along. Now I could see myself resisting every role that felt in any way like a box. I was going to have to find a way of knowing who I was that wouldn't limit me to roles.

- The new paradox of doing: If I could only be by doing, I could never sit down and enjoy the moment. I could continue doing many of the same things for a while, focusing my attention more on being in a better balance with doing. The continued need for challenges would be okay. I'd need to monitor the only-way-to-be-in-the-world need for goals or achievement.

- Feeling that the world had passed me by in small but telling ways: clinging to "You're welcome"; finding a stick-shift car an unappealing idea; no longer being able to tell one make and model of car from another; and worse yet, not being very interested in cars anymore. Needing more privacy and reflection in the midst of a life otherwise full of the trappings of extroversion; being at the stage of life, as my wife regularly points out, when younger women will not "get" my references to songs, wars, books, cars, or past politicians and political events; having lots of energy and opportunity for risk, with a corresponding awareness of fewer recuperative years than before if something went awry.

- Admitting that I no longer cared so much about the business I'd worked so hard to build; I no longer cared so deeply about a host of roles and proofs that until recently had been essential to my sense of identity and well-being. These still felt important, but had ceased to be the cornerstones of my life and identity.

- The realization that what had made me fairly successful in life until now—how I had created my identity and operated in the world, especially overcoming and seeking the next mountain—would need to be examined in a new light because some things could continue to serve me well after sixty but many would not.

- Appreciating that I had been at significant transition points before, but never at one of such apparently irreversible magnitude, and certainly never with such an array of experience, skills, relationships, and freedom to work with.

- Being joyfully willing to develop and sustain the skills and agility required for the next segment of my life.

- Carrying forward the best of my experience, identity, and ways of operating in the world.

- Discovering additional and more appropriate ways to create, be, and do in coming years.

- Integrating it all into a sense of self and capacity that can be validated by vitality and learning.

- Taking more conscious, active responsibility for myself and the quality of the life I'll live than anyone else will or should take.

The concept of a solid research project about all of this had been born. I wanted more understanding and ability. Only later did the idea of this book come into focus.

Upon our return home, I found myself searching San Francisco for a symbol, something that would capture the need for developing skills and agility. I found it on a rooftop billboard. I photographed it, marveling at the audacity and shallowness of the billboard's message—a challenge to everyone over fifty. If we believe the billboard, we're only alive when doing. If we're not doing, then we must be less than fully alive. Choice and degrees of doing aren't possible. This is unacceptable to me. The billboard said:

I DO. THEREFORE I AM.

I knew from my research interviews that what was happening to me was similar to what was happening for others—men and women alike. We have a huge desire to continue doing, and paradoxically, our reliance on doing as the sole way of being limits the quality of our lives in the long run. Will doing less mean we're dead? Is doing be our only way to feel alive? I'd found the symbol for skills and agility: bringing forward what would serve me well, leaving behind what wouldn't, and acquiring new, appropriate after-fifty abilities.

It's common before fifty for our identities to be 51 percent or more determined from outside the self: roles, achievement, work, family, attention, attachment, and intention have a heavy influence.

Example: Beth Allison, forty-seven, has devoted her life to her employer and her work, and has devoted herself equally to her children. She knows who she is: an employee part of the day and a mother part of the day. Her company is shutting down her office, and her last child is leaving for college. She won't fall apart, but neither will she be able to rely exclusively on those external ways of knowing who she is.

What begins to shift and end after fifty may be the very things that once gave life its greatest meaning. If we're paying attention, we'll discover that there may be a gradual change from being predominantly other-defined to predominantly self-defined. This shift is a cornerstone of the abilities we'll be working with later.

There's a coming demand for skills and agility for all of us. Members of the baby-boomer generation and people born shortly before and after comprise a cohort that's demonstrated a capacity for personal reinvention and changing the workplace, often successfully expecting that the world will change accordingly.

It might not be as simple as that in the future. Reinvention is often represented as leaving everything behind and starting anew. In fact, the finer and more successful forms of reinvention—according to everyone I interviewed—involve a combination of figuring out what to leave behind, what to bring forward, and what to start learning and experiencing that's new.

Skills and agility may require heightened attention and awareness in each moment as we go forth into the uncharted waters after-fifty.

Learning is important. Development is essential.
They aren't necessarily the same thing.

Chapter 2

Lifelong Learning and Lifelong Development Aren't Necessarily the Same Thing

Before moving into lifelong learning and development, it's important to ground ourselves in the basics of healthy aging. All the skills and agility we'll work with later can be directly tied to three key behaviors or characteristics. The better we are at directing our learning and development toward integrating these into our lives, the higher the quality of our lives can be.

Successful Aging by John Rowe, M.D. and Robert Kahn, Ph.D. advertises itself as "the most extensive, comprehensive study on aging in America." In "Toward A New Gerontology, The MacArthur Foundation Study of Successful Aging," they present:

> *Certainly freedom from disease and disability is an important component of successful aging. All of us have experienced the life-greeting euphoria, usually all too brief, that comes with recovery from illness, even a severe case of flu. But the absence of disease is not enough. A person who is not ill may nevertheless be at serious risk of illness or disability. And a person who is not at risk in those respects may be living a lonely and inactive old age. Our definition of successful aging takes account of all these facts.*
>
> *We therefore define successful aging as the ability to maintain three key behaviors or characteristics:*
>
> - *low risk of disease and disease-related disability;*
> - *high mental and physical function; and*
> - *active engagement with life.*

Each factor is important in itself, and to some extent inde-pendent of the others. Examples of this are all around us.

Drs. Rowe and Kahn give us a crucial insight: we need to pay attention to aging after fifty, but not make our lives primarily about aging. Acknowledging that each of their "three key be-haviors or characteristics" is "to some extent independent of the others" means acknowledging that they're also somewhat overlapping and interdependent.

As you read on, keep the three key behaviors or characteris-tics in mind. Which stories demonstrate their presence? Which demonstrate their absence? How do learning and development promote their presence?

Sara Crowe, fifty-four, lives in Arizona. Her husband, Ran-dy, shares her love of golf. Together, they exercise six times a week. They love to watch golf on TV. Their friendships are cen-tered at their golf club. It's the life they wanted and worked to have.

Roberta Salazar, sixty-three, lives in Ohio. Her husband died three years ago. She has devoted the past three years to politi-cal activities supporting legislation for the elderly. She sits on committees, fund-raises, speaks at the state capitol, and trav-els to conferences.

Sam Cohen, sixty-nine, lives in Los Angeles. He has devoted his life to his wife, his stores, and his children. Dorothy Co-hen is a social animal, and Sam relies on her for the couple's social life. For exercise they walk in their neighborhood ev-ery morning. Their children live on the East Coast. Sam and Dorothy have noticed that many of their friends are beginning to lose their health or spend more and more time in quieter places than LA.

As a result of being research participants, all of these peo-ple have deliberately moved into acquiring new vocabulary and knowledge and developing new abilities. They're paying more attention to the interdependent nature of The MacArthur

Foundation findings. They've begun to focus on lifelong learning and lifelong development. All of us after fifty will have to understand and be good at both to develop the necessary skills and agility.

By the time we're fifty, most of us have spent a lifetime learning and developing our preferred learning methods. We have a wealth of experience, knowledge, and information. By now we should all be experts in learning, but while all forms of learning are worthy, they're not all equal.

When we talk about learning, we're mostly talking about acquiring information. Also, you may have noticed that much of our learning attention goes to defining problems and creating solutions. Find the problem and solve it is our favorite kind of learning through doing. It's an expertise and a strength—until it's not.

Josie Greenwich, age fifty-five:
I'm tired of being the target of marketing campaigns that offer me solutions and relief from worries about everything from high blood pressure to financial planning to my assumed need for a carefree community of peers in which to live in my golden years. Clever people are building entire careers out of creating need and demand in a growing market with money: those of us over fifty. I know we need research; I'm glad people are anticipating our needs. But apparently we can't have research without hype, manufactured demand, and plenty of things to solve problems and worries I don't have. I'm going to have to be much more discerning and able than ever before to chart my own course and remain true to my own priorities.

What we haven't realized, and the people and companies selling us aging-related products and services won't tell us, is that aging isn't a problem that can be solved or moved beyond. Certainly, many aging-related aspects of our lives can be planned for, and one form of cosmetic solution or another purchased, but aging per se is not a problem. We're all going to discover that it's unavoidable, but in the end, aging isn't the point; the point is being great at living effective lives well beyond fifty.

As the baby boomers have approached and passed fifty, lifelong learning has become a popular, well-marketed niche creating wonderful opportunities for us to expand our horizons and explore our interests. For reasons we'll explore, lifelong development is less easily defined. It's also harder work for those who have the commitment and courage to pursue it.

The Critical Difference

The distinctions between lifelong learning and lifelong development require an examination of learning. While both "lifelongs" are essential to our quality of life, and overlap and complement each other, they're not the same. The quality of the learning often comes as much from the learner's reflection and subsequent possibilities as from the content of the experience.

Here are some important distinctions about learning:

Information: Data, facts, and images that can be recorded or memorized or stored. Information doesn't require a learner or knowledge; it requires a storage device, whether human, electronic, or paper. Information management is directly connected to moving facts and images around, but it's not necessarily connected to learning.

Example: The newspaper on your porch, the e-mail in your computer, the mail in your mailbox, the programs recorded on your Tivo, and dosage instructions on your prescription bottle—all are storage devices containing information. Your involvement as a learner isn't necessary for these devices and the information to exist.

Knowledge: Data, facts, images, and experience that a learner has integrated into his or her existing base of knowledge, thus upgrading integration, comprehension, usability, behavior, and perspective. Knowledge requires a learner and a knower.

Example: Let's say you've enrolled in a French class and a music appreciation class at a lifelong learning center. You're doing a lot of memorization work and a lot of practice. You're proud of your ability to order from a French menu, even prouder of your newfound knowledge of the history of classical music and theory of harmony.

Transformational Knowledge: Facts, images, and experience that are used to challenge the validity of a learner's existing base of knowledge, so the new knowledge can update or replace earlier wisdom, beliefs, and behaviors. From this challenge we create new possibilities. Transformational knowledge requires a higher level of learning expertise and awareness/reflection. It can be harder work. Transformational knowledge, applied, can be seen as increased skill.

Example: Ramon Phillips was recovering from an auto accident. It was the first time he'd been away from work for more than two weeks at a time in twenty-five years. The first week, he spent his time complaining, making his usually patient wife miserable. The second week, he phoned his workplace and made his employees miserable. The third week, he began to hear his own voice and the content of what he was saying. Ray said:

I'm not sure how it happened, but I realized I was devoting lots of energy to "Ain't it awful." I've been a really busy guy. Who had time to listen to himself? Now I had time. I didn't like what I heard, so I decided to start listening carefully to myself and to everyone else. The things I heard amazed me. Maybe the accident was some kind of gift. I'm being a lot nicer to my wife. Now I want to find a way to retain my gift of listening—and what I do about it—after I go back to work.

Lifelong Learning

Lifelong learning starts at birth. It involves repetition, content, attention, support, and use. We progress across our life spans to become adult learners who have several full sets of knowledge and are in a position to be 51 percent or more responsible for our own learning. We're learning how to avoid relying on the idea that learning has fixed endpoints. Information and knowledge are both fundamental to lifelong learning.

The Stairway of Lifelong Learning

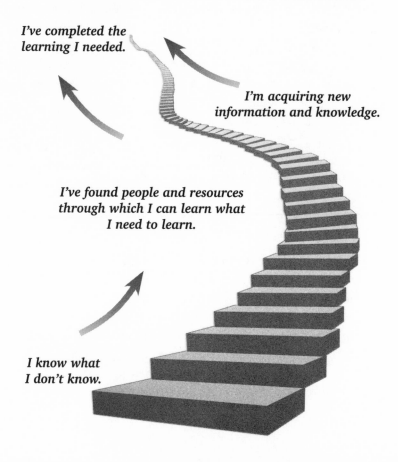

I've completed the learning I needed.

I'm acquiring new information and knowledge.

I've found people and resources through which I can learn what I need to learn.

I know what I don't know.

Example #1: Elizabeth is sixty-eight. She has a lifelong interest in Broadway theater, particularly the musical. Given the discretionary time since her retirement, Elizabeth has enrolled in a course entitled "History of the Broadway Musical" at a nearby lifelong learning center.

Example #2: Andy is fifty-eight. While he's not planning to retire, he's increasingly anxious about how he'll spend his time when he does. He hates having uncommitted time. Andy has enrolled in "Understanding the Stock Market," a course at a nearby community college.

Lifelong Development

Lifelong development also starts at birth. Development involves change, a combination of some things being carried forward, some new things being added, and some form of growth. Development is complex and experiential; it involves knowledge, facts, images, and experiences that are used to challenge the validity of the learner's existing base of knowledge, so the new knowledge can update and replace earlier wisdom, beliefs, and behaviors. Repetition, integration, and application of the learning are also part of lifelong development. Transformational knowledge requires a learner/knower.

The Stairway of Lifelong Development

I am applying the knowledge and insight to myself and the world around me.

I know I will find myself periodically back at the point where I don't know what I don't know.

I am assessing the validity of what I believed and knew in light of this new knowledge.

I am doing the learning.

I have clarity about what I don't know and clarity about what I need to learn.

I've found the people and resources.

I need to find the people and resources through which I can discover what I don't know.

I don't know what I don't know.

Example #1: Shelly Farber is sixty-six. Her husband died four years ago. Shelly knew she didn't want to spend the next part of her life in her neighborhood, so she took a two-year assignment as an ESL teacher in Thailand. Her intention was to greatly expand her sense of the world, and to form a new sense of self beyond the self she'd known and loved during all those years with her husband. Shelly concluded that she had to pursue lifelong development through experiences with people she didn't yet know.

Example #2: Rob and Thelma Thompson are both seventy-two and have always been "big-city folks." They're becoming more spiritually curious, and have enrolled in a two-week Elderhostel program on an Indian reservation in the Southwest. Knowing that temporarily changing locations is no guarantee of lifelong development, they remain committed to starting from "We don't know what we don't know." They've already concluded that they don't want to trash the life they're living, but don't want to continue limiting themselves to more of the same.

Lifelong learning and lifelong development are essential to our well-being. Usually, lifelong learning is easier, because it involves a higher proportion of memorization. Lifelong development is transformative, and will need to become a reliable component of skills and agility as our roads unfold. The smart knower/learner will be consciously capable of both.

What many of us practiced in our thirties and forties—juggling families, careers, education, membership in institutions important to what we sought to believe in, and achievement of goals that would prove our success and satisfaction to us and others—was development of the ability to hold multiple priorities, make good decisions while creating reliable space for others to live and grow in, and successfully climb the ladders of our choice. These lifelong learning and development abilities represented the top of the curve for previous generations.

From there it was often downhill into rest, retirement, loss, and death.

Now we're the ones who are fifty and beyond. What was true for previous generations isn't necessarily true for us. The knowledge we acquired and the ability we developed to put it to use in our thirties, forties, and fifties aren't the end for us, because our life spans extend out beyond the horizon of predictability. And change will happen relentlessly.

What we don't know—because never in history will so many people have lived so long or pioneered aging—is what we'll have to be good at. We do know that each previous period in our lives drove us toward abilities we'd need later. Why shouldn't that continue at fifty and beyond?

What's different this time

As we pass fifty we have the benefit of much more experience than before and, paradoxically, fewer years to recover from poor decisions, habit, and inertia.

What made us successful to this point might not be what will make us successful—or might even work against us—as we age.

We're going to experience an increasing amount of change and loss the older we become.

Our expectations of vitality and well-being are much higher than any previous generation's.

We'll need both lifelong learning and lifelong development to provide us with skills and agility if we're going to stay active and interacting effectively with our world.

We're more on our own to pioneer our lives after fifty than any generation before; we have freedom and personal responsibility for our lives that our parents' generation wouldn't have imagined with their institution-based definitions of retirement and aging based on role, age, gender, and retirement funding.

It will be important to understand and use the difference between information, knowledge, and transformative knowledge as we work with the abilities that are at the core of skills and agility after fifty.

Occasional disorientation may be an important cue that we should use our learning expertise and pay close attention.

The good news is that each year after fifty can be a great year. The surprising news is that, even with great planning, we'll have to pioneer them for ourselves one day and one year at a time.

Chapter 3

We Have Met the Pioneers
And They Are Us

During the interviews that inspired this book, many people expressed shock at the disappearance of the "Golden Years" they imagined their parents had enjoyed and they thought were their due. Many had grown up expecting that their parents' notions of retirement would apply to them also. A variety of causes demolished their cherished notions of golden years: need for more money; divorce; increased curiosity about the world; dissolution of long-term corporate employment with strong retirement systems; higher education levels; work as a significant source of validation; energy, structure, and social connection; deaths of peers; and disappearance of institution-sponsored models of coasting and slowly fading away.

Betsy Clingham, fifty-two, has continued to work as long as she and her husband, Bill, must pay college tuition for their children, but the end is in sight. Betsy plans to retire. Unlike several of her coworkers, she never considered her work a major part of her identity. While she'll feel no great loss in leaving work, Betsy is already feeling the loss of both the structure it has provided and the community it represented for years. Leaving work was always in her plan.

Phil Oshansky, seventy-two, has been a community activist for many years, serving on committees, commissions, and boards throughout his city. This year the mayor would like to promote him to a new commission, one expected to be highly political. For the first time in Phil's adult life, he isn't sure he's up to or wants the challenge. This wasn't in Phil's plan.

Carly Jeong is fifty-nine. She's a new grandmother, a regular volunteer at her church, and someone all her neighbors rely on if they are sick or lonely or traveling. Her church activities have led to an offer: would she like to spend a year abroad teaching others "less fortunate" what she knows about volunteering and service? This opportunity wasn't in Carly's plan.

Members of the baby-boomer generation—and those before and after them—form an extended cohort that has demonstrated a capacity for personal reinvention, changing their social environments, and reinventing their workplaces. They often expect that the world will continue to change for them. The baby boomers' collective biography is one of defining problems, creating solutions, and moving on. It might not be so simple as their cohort moves from being in control to exercising influence.

Why are we pioneers? Look around at the accelerating pace of change. See how different our expectations and realities are from those of our parents. Look closely at how important personal responsibility is going to be in crafting vital, meaningful lives for ourselves. Pioneering will be required of us if we're to succeed. It means entering territory that will be totally unfamiliar in some ways, territory that keeps changing, sometimes gradually, sometimes quickly. It means that we'll need to change and adapt with the new territory.

Example: Many of us who continue to work in "lifestyle jobs" (full- or part-time jobs that generate income and healthcare benefits but are no longer part of a career path, jobs intended instead to maintain our lifestyle after fifty) will work for managers twenty to thirty years our junior—some younger than our children. Succeeding at this will require some transformative learning on our parts and on the managers.

People often think of skills and agility as a kind of rubber-band-like stretching that returns eventually to its original shape. They also think of skills and agility as an ability to tough it out when times get rough. Actually, skills and agility are the ability to pay attention to experiences and learning, flexibly adopt what will be effective going forward, and expect that we'll never return exactly to the previous configuration. Life has moved on and so have we. Skills and agility can save us from the immobilization of disappointment and the pain of overreaction. They assume that the world, and we along with it, won't stay the same. Skills and agility are about dealing each day, directly and realistically, with what's happening in our lives. We'll need to ask regularly: "What is *really* going on here?"

Earlier generations lived and aged within agreed-upon norms of behavior and appearance for specific age groups. People understood what being ten or seventeen or thirty-five or in one's sixties or eighties should be. When youngsters acted childishly, parents told them, "Act your age." It was seldom necessary to say that to anyone over fifty.

Example: Mike Greenberg, seventy, bought his grandson, Ryan, a motorcycle. It was to be their shared project. All was well until Mike too started learning to ride the bike. Only Ryan thought Mike's riding was a great idea.

In 2000, 51 million Americans were between fifty and sixty-nine (US Census, issued October 2001). According to the Federal Interagency Forum on Aging Related Statistics, the key indicators of well-being for older Americans in 2000 were categorized by population, economics, health status, health risks and behaviors, and healthcare (www.agingstats.gov). For all the valuable studies and insights on aging, every statistic has a face, a biography, and the need for effective, capable aging behind it. By 2015 there'll be 77 million Americans between fifty and sixty-nine, many of them expecting to play, work, and live in significantly undiminished ways. The world of work is changing. More and more individuals are working from home offices at least part of each week. Companies are slowly awakening to the need to include workers over fifty-five in the "high potential" categories of top performers to invest in.

The problem is pretty clear. Workers will be harder to come by. Tacit knowledge will melt steadily away from your organization. And the most dramatic shortage of workers will hit the age group associated with leadership and customer-facing positions. Among those fifty-five and older who accepted early retirement offers, one-third have gone back to work. But these retirees are more likely to be working part-time or to be self-employed than their not-yet-retired counterparts—in other words, they're working on their own terms.

> Ken Dychtwald, Tamara Erickson, and Bob Morison,
> "It's Time to Retire Retirement,"
> *Harvard Business Review*, March 2004

We also have the arguments for and against older workers continuing to take jobs away from the younger generations who are entering the workforce, starting families, and being expected to foot the bill, through Social Security and other programs, for the support of people they'll never meet who are in competition with them for work and income. In 1940 there were forty-two workers paying into the Social Security system for every retiree taking money out. By 1950 there were just sixteen; it's projected that by 2030 there'll be only two.

When it comes to aging, we also point out that the United States is not alone. The entire developed world and large parts of the developing world, including China, are in the process of getting much older. This won't be a one-time event. The United States and its very best buddies will not only be getting old; they will be staying old.

> Laurence Kotlikoff and Scott Burns,
> *The Coming Generational Storm*

The past forty years have seen the alteration and disappearance of norms, expectations, and assumptions about aging—and the changes won't stop coming. This was consistently reflected in the stories my research participants told, and in the data they provided about relationships, identity, and demographics.

I designed the research to explore what key abilities people fifty and beyond would have to develop to have the skills and agility they'll need as they moved through their seventies, eighties, nineties, and beyond. No one group had answers for all, but every group had wisdom that could help everyone.

One common theme was the pleasure most participants took in their ability to greatly influence, if not control, their lives. Almost everyone saw him- or herself as having greater freedom than their parents' generation. Another consistent theme was some anxiety about the level of personal responsibility that accompanied the increased freedom.

One source of that freedom proved to be the dissolution of role-driven identities. Both men and women generally described satisfaction in living outside of strict expectations of what a man or woman should or shouldn't do because of age or gender. The sharing of household duties and income generation, along with assumptions of equal intellect, are thought to have increased the quality of life for everyone aged fifty and beyond.

Example: Dirk Vannett, sixty-four, had just retired. Dirk planned to devote himself to restoring classic cars. Instead, he volunteered to provide daycare for his new granddaughter two days a week. Millie Vanett, also sixty-four, decided she'd like to take a job for the first time in all the years she and Mike had been married. Taking a part-time job to start, she has developed career ambitions that extend out for the next ten years, including starting her own small business.

Another source of increased freedom arose from participants perceiving a large decrease in the impact of institutions, especially those that limit their focus to people who agree with them. Participants saw the norms of churches, companies employing workers, and entire communities as having less impact, except where these institutions have chosen to isolate themselves and limit change in the midst of our highly mobile society.

Hugely increased freedom was described in the many forms of interpersonal communication driven by education and access to information, travel, technologies, and expanding networks of people. Participants spoke of access to possibilities that would have been invisible to them—or nonexistent — earlier in history.

People are healthier than ever before. This, and the expectation of even more prolonged health and improved medical treatment, gave participants a freedom based in expectation and self-fulfilling prophecy. People simply no longer felt limited by the inevitability of disease. Those well beyond fifty described this as extending even further, through the development of lifelong learning in response to a greatly increased need for activity and personal effectiveness.

The great increase in education and affluence in our fifty-and-beyond population appears to have moved "personal reinvention" from an uncommon luxury to a cultural entitlement.

Finally, participants described a freedom to age in personally chosen ways as liberating and creating greatly diversified ways of aging.

Had the people you met in this chapter been of an earlier generation, they'd have had ready answers to their questions, had the questions arisen at all. There would have been prescribed gender-based roles and limitations for them. Such norms made everything simpler but left little room for freedom of choice. Instead, they're faced with creating solutions that work for them, inventing models as they go—often, the price of freedom is responsibility.

We no longer agree on what "old" is. Stereotypical images survive, tied to obsolete models of age-specific behavior, belief, and appearance. Loss, disease, dependence, financial incapacity, and lack of "productivity" are often our focus when we speak of "the elderly." It's no surprise that much of the current gerontologic literature focuses on physical and psychological health, financial planning, estate and tax planning, and social activity.

Assuming that development and aging are lifelong, then maturation and aging blend over time into a very personal process as well as a shared social process. Successful maturation and aging requires competence, individually and socially. Competencies acquired earlier in life might serve well after fifty, or might not, or might get in the way. Competencies not already developed might need to be acquired early enough—in one's sixties, for example—that they're available for practice when they're really needed, say in one's eighties.

Individually and collectively, we're free of the powerful financial, institutional, and social standards that used to direct our ideas about life after fifty. We also have the unprecedented individual responsibility for finding ways of aging that will work for us.

People now beyond fifty have every expectation of remaining actively engaged in the world. With "elderly" on their distant horizons—and no longer so chronologically based—they know that their capacity to "do" will inevitably diminish over time. For many, such a diminution of driven-ness will be a relief; for others it will be a substantial loss, associated with diminished vitality.

All these circumstances set us up to be pioneers. We'll pioneer our own lives and the way we live them. How well we acquire and exercise our abilities after fifty will determine how successful we are in building sustainable skills and agility for the rest of our lives.

The best plans aren't carved in stone.
They are written down and edited thoughtfully
every day of our lives.

Chapter 4

Life Often Doesn't Go According to Plan. Planning Is Essential Anyway

Planning has been a leading force throughout human evolution, as well as an intrinsic element in meaning-making, individual effectiveness, and cultural development.

Without planning and preparation our ancestors wouldn't have been able to feed and shelter and protect the family. Communities worshipped the seasons and relied on their cyclical dependability as the structure on which beliefs, societal norms, and rituals could be hung as evidence of cohesion and stability.

It is estimated that in the forty-five hundred years from the Bronze Age to the year 1900, life expectancy increased twenty-seven years, and that in the short period from 1900 to 1990 it has increased by at least that much. The changes have been so dramatic that it is currently estimated that of all human beings who have ever lived to be sixty-five years or older, half are currently alive. (John Rowe and Robert Kahn, "Toward A New Gerontology, The MacArthur Foundation Study of Successful Aging," 1998.)

It's easy to argue that in many ways planning started out as common sense created by people who paid attention; fundamental requirements of survival in a relatively steady world with low levels of change and high predictability.

It's as easy to argue that we've progressed into a world of increasing change, decreasing predictability, and unparalleled need for specialized knowledge: medicine, nutrition, financial management, law, technologies, banking, and communications.

In a World Future Society article on The Cyber Future, *Futurist* editor Edward Cornish cites ninety-three ways in which our lives will change by 2025, including:

- Education may become compulsory for adults as well as children.

- Skills and knowledge will become obsolete faster than ever.

- InfoTech will take over far more jobs for which humans were once thought indispensable.

- People will do most of their financial business on computers at home.

- The increasing complexity of the global financial system will make it highly vulnerable to disruption.

- Government officials and dissidents will increasingly use cyberspace to spread lies as well as accurate information.

- People's attention may become the world's most precious resource.

- Awesome possibilities for self-knowledge will open up.

The planning horizon is shortening, creating an even greater need for intelligent planning, monitoring progress, and the ability to flex, abandon plan, and respond creatively in the moment.

If you have any doubt about the place of planning in our society—and its financial power in the marketplace, go to your favorite search engine, enter the word "planning," and see how many websites are listed. My search yielded 1,770,000,000. How could one sort through so many?

Planning is crucial for us individually and as a society. In our busy world of specialized knowledge and rapid change, planning is vital to our sense of stability, identity, effectiveness, and control.

What constitutes effective planning? Many futurists say that most planning is an extrapolation of the past and the present, and rather than planning the future, we're actually planning an improved past and present. Financial planners usually ask four questions: (1) When do you want to retire? (2) How much money will you need to live the life you imagine for yourself? (3) What will it take for you to get from where you are now to where the plan says you'll need to be? (4) How soon would you like to start? Assuming we can accurately describe the life we imagine for ourselves, quantitative financial plans are easy to create and follow. The life we imagine for ourselves, however, may be a moving target.

According to Jane Bryant Quinn, "In fifteen years, the normal retirement age will be 70 or more, because that's what it's going to take to keep your lifestyle high, bills paid, and wallet full." (*Newsweek,* July 21, 2003.)

How about career planning? After fifty? You bet. To avoid becoming a generation of Wal-Mart greeters, middle-aged baby boomers have to plan. It's easier to keep a job at sixty-five than to look for one at seventy-five, when money is starting to worry you. People after fifty and well beyond are pioneering, discovering the joys of giving up balancing their work and personal lives. Instead, they're integrating the two, doing far more telecommuting, buying houses with home office space, and bridging the gap between full-time work and full-time retirement.

NOTE: Your career professional should understand the difference between Job Search (finding the next job) and Career Management (the ongoing effort to match your stage of life and current/future needs with the content and configuration of your work life). If your career professional can't make the distinction, find one who can.

Phil Turner said:

I've decided to get a real estate license. I've always been interested in residential real estate. My partner, Barry, and I

can't both be home all day. One or the other of us has to be
busy out of the house most days. I wish I'd planned better,
but I didn't know I'd still have all this energy. We know a lot
of people who'll want to sell their houses here to get away
from our cold climate. A lot of them will move to a warmer
climate and buy homes. If Barry and I work it right, I can help
people sell their homes here in the spring and summer, and
we can move ourselves seasonally to a warmer place where I
can help them buy their new homes. Sounds perfect to me. I
wish I'd thought it through earlier. And I'm only sixty-two.

Healthcare planning—at least the non-financial part of it—is
another matter. What was your parents' health history? What can
we predict yours will be? Will you outlive your spouse? Will your
children be available to care for you? There's often a wide gap
between imagining the future and accurately predicting it.

How about social activity planning, a selling feature of many
"adult residential communities," lifelong learning organizations,
and partner-finding websites. When is planning really planning,
and when is it simply an accumulation of possibilities?

And how much planning is enough? It's as individual as
fingerprints.

About Planning and Fear

What remains to discuss about planning and the
planning industry is its darker side: the sale of solutions to
imagined problems, and the sale of hope and relief from fear,
which are often key ingredients in planning. The problems
arise when we're unaware that hope and fear have become
dominant factors in the marketing strategies directed at us,
and become our reasons for buying planning services. Fear is
incorporated into the headlines of problem/solution publications, TV shows and advertising, Internet pop-ups, and every
other form of communication bombarding us each day. Go to

a newsstand and really examine the cover titles on the major magazines. or really listen to a series of TV commercials. How many use anxiety to boost sales? The pitches play to various fears: fear of never having or being; of having and losing; of not measuring up; of missing out; of criticism; of what will happen if we don't plan enough; of not fitting in; of nasty surprises—the list is endless.

Phil Andrewski, fifty-five, often wakes at 2 a.m., terribly worried about his future. He's not as far ahead financially as he thought he'd be by now. His small architectural firm is successful, but the effort of keeping clients and staff happy and completing projects on time is draining him emotionally and physically. Also, he's tired of feeling underpaid in comparison to the work required to keep everything going well. Employees he used to prize are beginning to feel like weights. Phil knows he needs to provide better for his wife, Janice, but he's not feeling very creative and feels like he's running out of time. Phil's experience was disturbingly common in my research.

The problem/solution motif is incorporated into the planning industry's marketing because of how we live in this fast-moving, information-based—not necessarily knowledge-based—society. Hope and fear are built into the very structure of how we give and receive communication at work and at home, normalized to the point where we hardly notice it, if at all.

As a famous comic-strip villain said, "The more fear you make, the more loot you take."

The popular antidotes to problems and fear are solutions and hope. Problems and solutions attract attention, sell hope for avoiding whatever anxiety or fear has been provoked, and generate big bucks. Fear starts—and is required for—many sales cycles. Please, do a reality check for yourself before you buy, invest, or hire. Not an indictment of the planning industry, this is a plea to you: find the right advisors and never let them take more responsibility for you and your future than you take yourself.

You must know and live every day with ten realities of life after fifty.

10 Key Realities After Fifty

1. Planning is essential.

2. The pace of change is accelerating.

3. No one's life happens completely according to plan.

4. Thriving beyond fifty requires special abilities.

5. The path we expect will change as it unfolds before us.

6. What we were good at in the past may not be what we'll need to be good at in the future. In fact what we were good at can become an obstacle.

7. Our situations and companions will change as we age, often without notice.

8. Aging can't be solved nor moved beyond like a problem.

9. Acquiring and practicing the right abilities early will make a difference in the quality of life each day after fifty.

10. There's no one-size-fits-all answer for thriving after fifty. Success requires awareness and resilience in taking daily responsibility for ourselves.

Everyone fifty and beyond needs a set of complete, flexible, periodically updated plans. Which kinds are essential, how often they need to be updated, the role of hope and fear in planning, and the degree to which the plans form a clear map leading to relatively stable and predictable places is "as individual as fingerprints."

Planning starts at home. What's true about your life now? What would you like to keep? What would you like to replace? What haven't you done that you'd like to do? Who haven't you been but would like to be? How can you get from here to there?

You're free to buy or hire all the planning tools and resources you need. In the end, only you can be responsible for your planning, knowing when it's enough, editing your plan regularly, and building the skill and agility you'll need when life inevitably doesn't go according to plan.

Planning is essential, but if we're not careful, it becomes just an improved extension of past and present rather than a true future plan. Having a plan does not eliminate freedom of choice.

Everyone fifty and beyond needs a set of flexible skills, practiced and continually developed, that will enable them to be agile whether events happen inside or outside of plan.

Ability usually takes practice.

Chapter 5

A New Framework for Skill and Agility After Fifty

You've met a number of interview participants, most of them "average" people doing the best they can. Given the opportunity to speak privately and at length, many were thoughtful and articulate about life after fifty. In analyzing the interviews and hard data about each participant, I found that all the people whose past-fifty lives the participants admired had needed to become great at exercising four key abilities. The participants themselves had already come to expect—though they didn't know each other or express it in shared vocabulary—that they too would need to be good at these four abilities.

The participants had new information for us. Reciting (memorizing and repeating) a list of the four isn't enough. Understanding and practicing (transformation of thinking, possibility, and behavior) the four soon after fifty, and continuing to do so into elderhood, could help us develop the essential high mental functioning and engagement with life.

The Four Abilities and Their Corollary Personal Responsibilities

Identity Ability is the ability to adapt our identity to meet current circumstances and needs as our lives change. Working with *identity anchors* as tools lets us get quickly to the heart of the matter. The *corollary responsibility* is our obligation to create identities that promote our internal sense of wholeness (how we feel about ourselves regardless of the world around us) and our external sense of integrity and ability (how we feel about our place and competence in the world).

Meaning-making Ability is the ability to be aware of and choose the meaning we make of events, and to tell stories about them to ourselves and others in any way we choose. The corollaries are: (1) Responsibility for telling the story as accurately as we can; and (2) Responsibility for the impact of the stories we tell (including to ourselves) on our own and others' behavior and beliefs.

Community Ability is the ability to select and build the communities we belong to, cultivate the relationships we need to invest time and energy in, and focus on the characteristics we find acceptable in, and require of, those communities and relationships. The corollary responsibility is continuing to manage and update our community memberships and our relationships within them so we have the right balance (what "right balance" is can change over time for each of us) between the connections that are familiar, stable, and efficient, and those that are unfamiliar and full of new ideas and information.

Selecting Ability is the ability to make best-fit, informed choices for ourselves, alone and with the help of others. After-fifty choices are likely to require thinking and selecting beyond the yes/no choices we made earlier in our lives. These selections are more likely to require understanding the dynamic tensions of the situation and choosing the best solutions or compromises among myriad possibilities. They also tend not to stay made, requiring later re-selection. The corollaries are: (1) Responsibility for deciding (not to choose is to choose) in a timely, informed fashion; and (2) Being more responsible for our decisions than any one else is, until we're ready to relinquish primary responsibility for our decision making to someone else.

Understanding and practicing these abilities after fifty is an exercise in lifelong learning and lifelong development.

Practicing them well can lead to skills and agility. Taking personal responsibility one day at a time, and focusing energy on high mental functioning and engagement with life, are key. Imagine a life without understanding and exercising these abilities, and you'll begin to see the difference between focusing on clinging to the status quo and focusing on having a truly agile life each day beyond fifty.

Events happen: spiritual awakenings, financial downturns, retirement, death of loved ones, new work opportunities, residential moves, new friendships, health problems, travel, education, and changes and losses spaced very closely. Look at your life and imagine these four abilities in place as filtering devices through which you can work in a skillful, agile way.

What follows is a model of the flow of our daily lives. First, events happen. Sometimes we call them to us: we take a trip or invite neighbors over for dinner. Sometimes they can be imposed on us: we receive difficult news or get involved in a traffic accident. They can happen directly to us or we can observe other people's events. We're not always in control of events, but we have great personal freedom in how we anticipate and respond to them. As soon as we acknowledge needing or having the necessary skills and agility, we must also accept their corollary responsibilities.

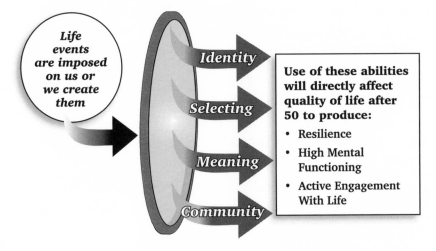

Imagine this model in place in your life as a skill-and-agility filtering device through which you can be free (assuming you're also willing to be responsible) to work with all the events that occur in your life. In the next chapters, you'll explore each of the four abilities in detail, and meet new companions on the unfolding road. You'll have the opportunity to work with their stories in a series of exercises that will help you understand each story in different ways. The process may transform your own story and expand your capacity for skill and agility after fifty.

As part of our learning in these next chapters, we'll connect four important points, allowing us to more fully understand each situation and person.

- The first point is the three Truths (pages 3–5).
- The second point is the ten Realities (page 52).
- The third point is our analysis of the person's key ability in each chapter.
- The fourth point is any evidence of the person's willingness to assume the corollary responsibilities.
- We'll use this approach in all the remaining chapters, where our learning opportunities lie in understanding each person's story and key abilities. Please keep your notebook handy, and write all your answers in it.

Changing your identity does not mean dishonoring who you were. It means being very real about who you need to be now.

Chapter 6

Identity Ability:
Who You've Been May Not Be
Who You'll Need to Be

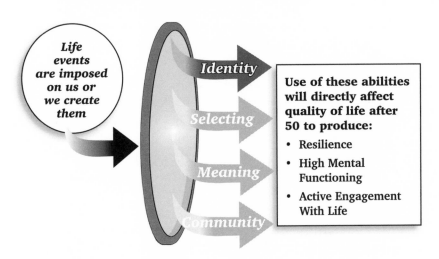

Life events are imposed on us or we create them

Identity

Selecting

Meaning

Community

Use of these abilities will directly affect quality of life after 50 to produce:

- Resilience
- High Mental Functioning
- Active Engagement With Life

Identity: The word looks simple enough. Who am I? How did I get to be who I am? I like who I am, so why should I change? Who will I need to be in the future? From a lifelong-development standpoint, identity evolves with the ongoing crafting of our unfolding lives. For many people fifty and beyond, the notion that we grow tall and then just continue to be more of the same no longer rings true.

Explore identity, however, and you'll discover that it's much more complicated. "Who am I?" is a central, shared experience of humankind. It begins early in our lives with: (1) What we're told or shown by others; (2) Comparing ourselves to something or someone else; and (3) The conclusions we draw about ourselves from experience.

Ron Kelly, seventy-two, was a late-in-life baby his parents didn't want, and they took no pains to hide it. Despite having lived a rich, full life, the sense of being an unwanted child remains at least a small part of Ron's identity.

Bertha Kellogg, forty-three, has always been naturally blonde, unusually pretty, and graceful. Beauty opened lots of doors for her, as she and others continually compared her appearance to that of other girls.

Sometimes our identities are challenged when the world won't behave the way we expect. Frieda Moore, fifty-one, recently requested that I do career work with her twenty-two-year-old, Brad, a recent college graduate. Brad majored in history, but doesn't want to teach school, and Frieda thinks he's not as active as he should be in "deciding what he's going to do and getting a job at it." My listening to Frieda disclosed something she hadn't admitted, even to herself:

"Tom and I raised him, fed him, clothed him, and educated him. I want some closure, I want him settled. It's the best way I'll know I've been a good mother."

My standard question when I receive calls like Frieda's: "Whose need are we meeting here?" Through my own sons, I understand the challenge to my identity when they don't act according to my plan. But, there's a far more effective way for people Brad's age to begin and manage a career than to choose what they're going to do professionally for the rest of their lives, especially if supporting their parents' identities is a primary driver. Also, especially after fifty, there's a more thoughtful and self-dependent way for parents to know who they are after their kids have left the nest.

There are periods in our lives when we're less clear about who we are than we like to be. Before fifty, it's common for our identities to be 51 percent or more determined from outside the self. Roles, achievement, work, family, attention, attachment, and intention have a heavy external influence earlier in life. This may or not continue as we pass fifty, depending on our preferences and our ability to reflect on what's really going on. After forty and fifty in my life and the lives of many of my research participants, what began to shift and/or end were the very things that earlier gave our lives their greatest meaning.

One of the keys to working with identity ability is *identity anchors*—the foundations of how we maintain the ability to manage our sense of who we are. We can anchor our sense of ourselves to places, things, values, personal traits, abilities, relationships, interests, and priorities. For most of us, our identities don't remain fixed; they evolve with us across our life spans. Some anchors may remain fixed, unless we choose to release them, but most serve for a limited time and then lose their relevance. The world changes, we change, our interactions change, and our identities adapt accordingly.

It's easy to make a long list of things that define who we are. It's harder—and more rewarding —to identify those key anchors that are at the core of who we think we are and how we operate in the world.

Two aspects are central to understanding identity anchors.

1. They serve to keep something safe and centered, but simultaneously prevent that thing from moving on even if it needs to—a bit of a paradox.

2. They have their own strengths and characteristics that are often in opposition to the strength and force of change that may be trying to dislodge them.

Identity anchors share these two aspects with other types of anchors. Two major forces working on identity anchors are *belonging*—the need to know who am I when I'm with others and how successful I am at maintaining the level of belonging I think I should have—and *individuation,* the need to know who am I and how successful I am at being an independent individual regardless of the forces of belonging. We always have the need for *enough* belonging or sense of ourselves as having community membership and similarity with others. And, we always have the need for *enough* individuation or sense of ourselves as separate beings. How much is enough is a personal choice, and the mix of the two rarely remains constant throughout our lives. The tension between belonging and individuation, and our movement between them, can be key drivers of our development. Both needs are always present; either can dominate for a while and then relinquish dominance to the other.

Sometimes, belonging dominates. Our identity anchors are tugged this way and that, at times changing, at times remaining intact. We can pay a heavy price for the right to belong. Starting with adulthood, many of us strive to create identities dominated by roles, a strong form of belonging: parent, employee, husband, wife, and homeowner. At other times, individuation dominates, precipitating periods like the misleadingly (and regrettably, for a perfectly natural transition) named "midlife crisis." Again our identity anchors come under pressure. At the extreme in individuation, we spend enormous energy challenging what we've built to date, and calling into question what we thought we knew and what others believed about us. The "terrible twos," some of the teenage years, and midlife crisis are usually driven at least in part by individuation.

All of this is normal and expected in the course of each individual's development. Scholars have found it impossible to create stages that include all factors every time. All-inclusive stage theories exist, and we can find examples that prove each, but we can also find examples that blow each theory to bits. Regardless of what the stage theorists propose, belonging and individuation are very personal matters throughout life.

Previous generations believed that identity was complete about the time one reached full physical height. Who you were by then was who you'd be for the rest of your life. Today we know that's not true. Who we are—who we create ourselves to be—should change over time because our lives change and so might our environment.

The key to making a successful identity change lies in first figuring out, as clearly and certainly as possible, who we really are and who we really want to be, and then using that knowledge to gradually create the needed changes.

Identity change has spawned major industries, all derived from the need for it, anxiety about it, and wanting to get it "right." Therapies, the search for your "true self," the call for personal "reinvention," finding the "child within," or awakening your "unrealized potential," are too often rooted in and sold from a problem/solution perspective that uses fear as a motivator while offering hope of significant change. Many of these services and products have the potential to be positive and healthy, while many are nothing but shams.

Going through any kind of introspective change process after fifty, it's important to keep an eye on our motivations, needs, and goals. It's equally important to have people in our lives who understand and appreciate the efforts we're making and who serve as strong, lasting sounding boards for us.

As our lives unfold in a complex, fast-paced world, it is appropriate for us not only to take on new traits but also to enlarge and redefine our sense of self. Continual self-redefinition is increasingly recognized to be a normal element of healthy adult development.

William A. Sadler, *The Third Age*

At fifty and beyond, you have the ability and the right to evaluate, change, and retain your identity(ies) and how you use it (them) in the world. The research participants who contributed to this book took a pragmatic approach. They said, "I have a wide range of temporary identities. I can be slightly or dramatically different depending on the social environment and my mood.

What matters is my *home identity base,* which remains constant regardless of temporary, externally driven change. These anchors of my identity serve as the core of how I think of myself and how I operate. I can diverge from them in any given situation, but they're what I return to."

For some, the identity anchors were predominantly belonging-oriented; for others, primarily individuation-oriented. There's no right answer or balance, and what answers we have will change periodically as we advance beyond fifty.

Identity ability allows people after fifty to adapt their identity (their anchors and how they vary from them, depending on situation) to meet the new circumstances and events that become part of maturing, living a full biography, and aging. Exercising this freedom now develops the skills and agility that are essential later as "elderly" approaches. We're free to assume identity ability's corollary responsibility: to create identities that promote our internal sense of wholeness and our external sense of integrity. This paired freedom and responsibility requires understanding and working with our identity anchors regularly.

David Paulson

- **Age:** Sixty
- **Residence:** San Francisco, California
- **Work:** Commercial real estate broker
- **Marital Status:** Married thirty-four years; wife Diane
- Major fear about aging after fifty: Becoming an impoverished male "bag lady."
- **Major daily struggle after fifty:** Waiting for the other shoe to drop in a negative way.
- **Major surprise about life after fifty:** Feeling consistently more relaxed than I expected to feel.

David has had several careers and many jobs, and has lived in a number of large cities. About five feet, eight inches tall, with a full head of silver-blonde hair, a big smile, and earnest blue eyes, David is a cancer survivor—five years now. And not just any cancer survivor, a "poster boy," even at work. He has been married for thirty-four years. Early in life he decided he was a good person but would—based on experience and observing others—reject organized religion. David and his wife, Diane, have developed a plan for the next ten to fifteen years, "Before it's too late," as they put it. They'll need to watch their money closely, but their plan is workable: Work part of the time, travel part of the time, enjoy San Francisco and friends part of the time. David says, "I like to think we're unique among our friends, and as determined to chart our own destiny as it's possible to be. We may not live up to it all the time, but it's the way I believe in operating."

As dedicated as David is to cancer research, and as much good as he's done for others, he can't imagine making his poster-boy status the focus of his identity for the rest of his life. Except for his marriage, which has provided the stability that allowed him to live the life he has lived, his biography is one of total dedication and then moving on to the next thing. He and Diane threw a party to launch their plan and themselves. "I love life," he kept saying to their friends. They leased their condo for six months to a visiting professor. Two weeks later, just as they were packing for a trip to China, Diane found a lump in her breast.

They canceled their trip and arranged to take possession of their condo again. Diane has already begun chemotherapy. It's not only their immediate world that has changed; if Diane doesn't survive her cancer, David's long-term world will change even more dramatically.

We know that David's self-identified identity anchors are:

CANCER SURVIVOR   GOOD HUSBAND
SAMPLER AND TASTER OF LIFE
STANFORD GRADUATE   NON-RELIGIOUS

Analysis

(*from here on, write your answers in your notebook*):

- Of the three Truths (pages 3–5), which ones are important in David's situation?

- Of the ten Realities (page 52), which ones are important in David's situation?

- Analysis of David's identity ability: How will David's current identity anchors be helpful to him? How could they be a hindrance to him?

- Evidence of David's willingness to assume the corollary responsibilities.

Amy Corbin

- **Age:** Sixty-three
- **Residence:** Baltimore, Maryland
- **Work:** Philanthropic activities, especially volunteer fundraising for non-profits
- **Marital Status:** Divorced (eight years ago)
- **Children:** Kevin, age forty; Susan, thirty-eight; four grandchildren
- **Major fear about aging after fifty:** "Losing my independence."
- Major surprise about life after fifty: "Living alone and really liking it, something I'd often wondered about but never expected to do."

Amy devotes her energies to fundraising for causes she believes in. Divorced at fifty-five after thirty-two years of marriage,

Amy lives in Baltimore. Tall and dignified, she prefers tailored clothes and minimal jewelry with maximum impact. Amy has a great financial planner, and her divorce left her in the position of not having to work. When one of Amy's grandchildren asked Amy to roll down the hilly lawn with her one day, Amy did. Embarrassed by the two of them rolling down the lawn, Amy's daughter, Susan, yelled, "For God's sake, Mother, act your age!"

"I don't know what acting my age looks like anymore, but I don't like your definition," Amy yelled back. What stung her much more than her daughter's viewpoint was Amy's realization that she had rejected most of the definitions of aging she was accustomed to, but hadn't thought to replace them with anything other than daily living. "I'm not that different from other people. My life has in many ways been decided for me while my back was turned, regardless of my planning. I work with that by having a very clear idea of who I am and who I need to be. It's not necessarily a natural thing for me to do, but I've done it for years and partially reinvented myself more than a few times now."

Beginning to weary of being exclusively in philanthropic efforts and circles, Amy is considering going back to work for the first time in thirty-five years. She says, "At first I thought I'd engage in lifelong learning programs, but the ones I found were more about entertainment or daily health—everything from "The History of the Broadway Musical" to "Yoga for Seniors"—than about lifelong learning about self and personal effectiveness in the world. My friends who participated in your research found it so thought-provoking that they talked me into doing this. As soon as I filled out your survey I understood this was an opportunity for me. It wasn't easy, and I'm very careful about my time, but nobody for a long time has pushed my head around the way your survey did. I want to develop as a person in my mid-sixties, not memorize interesting but non-developmental information. I need to find someplace that takes my need for professional and personal growth as seriously as I do. Should I find a job, or start my own business?"

Amy is clear that she needs to expand her circle of friends and acquaintances at a time when most people's circles are shrinking through retirement, illness, death, the absence of children's shared activities as a social bonding agent, and relocation to warmer climates.

We know that Amy's self-identified identity anchors are:

SELF-RELIANT (TO THE POINT OF SOMETIMES BEING A "LONER")
EXTREMELY ABLE   MOTHER AND GRANDMOTHER
INQUISITIVE   CITIZEN OF BALTIMORE

Analysis:

- Of the three Truths (pages 3–5), which ones are important in Amy's situation?

- Of the ten Realities (page 52), which ones are important in Amy's situation?

- Analysis of Amy's identity ability: How will Amy's current identity anchors be helpful to her? How could they be a hindrance to her?

- Evidence of Amy's willingness to assume the corollary responsibilities.

Chuck DiJulio

- **Age:** Forty-eight

- **Residence:** Princeton, New Jersey

- **Work:** President, DiJulio Construction, a remodeling business

- **Marital Status:** Remarried, ten years (divorced at thirty-seven after fifteen years of marriage); wife: Diane

- **Children:** Tom, age twenty-five; Steve, twenty-four; Christy, ten; two grandchildren

- **Major fear about aging after fifty:** "I love my business, but I'm afraid Diane and I won't ever have the time to enjoy the fruits of our hard work building and running this business."

- **Major daily struggle after fifty:** Continuing to do dangerous physical things on construction sites and when I'm working in the yard—as if I didn't know I'm not eighteen anymore.

Chuck owns a successful home-remodeling business. He lives and works in the Princeton area. He's a large man, with a relaxing presence and a ready smile. He often runs his fingers through his hair, a long-standing habit when he's thinking deeply.

Chuck imagined for years that he'd be retired by now, his children long gone, and golf his major interest. Something intervened: he divorced his first wife because "To tell you the truth, we couldn't stand it anymore."

Chuck thinks his divorce was the greatest gift of his life. It challenged everything about who he thought he was, opened his eyes to "really building" his own business, created the space for Diane, his current wife, to come into his life, and led to the birth of his daughter Christy. Chuck and Diane are both active in running the business daily. Chuck's friends from Rotary, church, community boards, and professional associations, mostly entrepreneurs like Chuck, have nearly all "made it" and sold their businesses. Chuck has had to make almost all new business friendships while trying to stay connected with his old friends.

Chuck's social life is dominated by the generation behind him, whose young children will still be at home for a long time. He's going to get a very late start doing what he thinks of as "normal later-in-life things"—if he ever gets to do them at all.

Chuck and Diane DiJulio have their feet in two worlds, the world of their business and daughter, and the world they imagine for themselves eight years from now, when Christy is in college and they've sold the business. They envision things they haven't done: travel the world, explore the arts, spend a lot of time in New York City, and learn creative computer technologies.

We know that Chuck's self-identified identity anchors are:

STEADY AND RELIABLE   GOOD FATHER AND HUSBAND
PROFESSIONAL BUILDER AND REMODELER
COMMUNITY VOLUNTEER   PEOPLE PERSON

Analysis:

- Of the three Truths (pages 3–5), which ones are important in Chuck's situation?
- Of the ten Realities (page 52), which ones are important in Chuck's situation?
- Analysis of Chuck's identity ability: How will Chuck's current identity anchors be helpful to him? How could they be a hindrance to him?
- Evidence of Chuck's willingness to assume the corollary responsibilities.

*Not all the stories we tell and hear
serve us well or remain true forever.*

Chapter 7

Meaning-making Ability:
We Become the Stories
We Tell and Hear

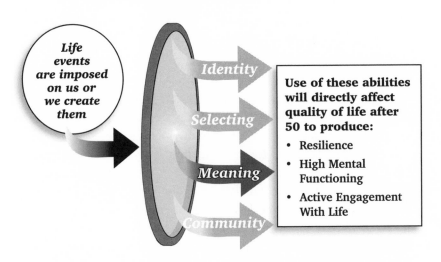

As children we loved stories. As adults we're very fond of them,
too. They come in wrappers: books, TV, conversations with
neighbors, discussions at work, morality stories at school and
church, newspapers and magazines, the Internet, and e-mail.
One of my personal heroes, Studs Terkel, has built a whole
identity and reputation (another form of story) by doing a
fantastic job of collecting stories and making them available to
us in his books. We all tell stories and listen to them throughout
every day of our lives, even when we're alone.

In all my books , my informants—mostly the uncelebrated, heroes of the ordinary—had recounted, in their own words, the lives they had lived, the epochs they had survived.... In recalling actual experiences, my colleagues, the true authors of these works, found their own eloquence and poetry. Words from the seemingly inarticulate flowed like wine. At times they were as astonished as I was.

Studs Terkel, *Will The Circle Be Unbroken?*

Reflections on Death, Rebirth, and Hunger for a Faith

Try observing something. It can be anything: having your first cup of coffee in the morning, overhearing your boss chew someone out at work, or watching people stand up on the bus or change lanes on the freeway quickly without signaling. Now, try to store that experience in your head without using words or an image. Can you do it? Not likely, because our brains work with symbols, whether words or images or both. Now, try to store that same experience in your head using whatever words and images work for you. Can you do it? Sure, because you're working with your brain the way it likes to work.

Those packets of words and images we store—whether from what we've directly observed or experienced or what has been related to us by others—are the stories we keep and tell to ourselves and others in various forms, over and over. Eventually, we've told them so often they are truth to us and are therefore what we believe. This process of observation or receiving information followed by word and image storage is the process of making meaning. Over time we become the stories we save and tell.

In his bestseller, *Awaken The Giant Within: How to Take Immediate Control of Your Mental, Emotional, Physical, and Financial*

Destiny!, Tony Robbins devotes chapters to belief, vocabulary, and the power of life metaphors. He does this because he understands the importance and impact of the stories we tell ourselves and others. From Tony's book:

> *Realize, believe, and trust that if you change the meaning of any event in your mind, you will immediately change how you feel and what you will do, which will lead you to change your actions and thus transform your destiny.*

It seems a huge leap to go from examining belief to arriving at control and success. I wonder about the important distinction between absolute control and informed, powerful influence. How many readers see and work with this important distinction in analyzing the meaning of events?

It doesn't seem a huge leap to understand that examining the stories we store and become can free us to consider other possibilities. For people fifty and beyond, this examination and the courage to take responsibility is an essential freedom. From exercising this freedom can come skills and agility.

Our lives are getting busier. Lots of fully retired people told me that they wondered, in retrospect, how they'd ever found time to work. People still working full-time are juggling multiple priorities. We're bombarded by messages—phone, e-mail, mail, TV, etc.—and often pour as much time into selecting what we're going to pay attention to as we used to spend paying attention. It's no wonder we like our information in pill form: sound bites, three-sentence e-mails, short voice-mail messages, postcards, and best of all, lists.

Books and other forms of publications have adopted lists as a selling feature. There are books made up entirely of lists, and many books with pseudonyms for lists: habits, steps, principles, secrets, rules, etc. In the midst of our busy lives, these lists all help us condense information, which in turn helps us more quickly choose the words and images we need to form the stories we'll retain and become. When it comes to making meaning, we have only so much attention to spread around. The danger is, of course, that other people's lists can become a substitute for our ability to think. Nonetheless, we *love* lists. And why not? They come to us with the images and words already preformed. All we have to do is add our own details.

Busy as you may be beyond fifty, it's time to pay attention to what's in your mental warehouse and what you're creating to put into brain storage each day. You are the words and images you store and the stories you tell yourself and others. By the time we're fifty, we've stored a whole lot of words and images in our heads as stories. Some of them are accurate and will continue to serve us well. Some were never accurate. Some never served us well at all. The same holds true for the stories we create today while we're busy doing other things.

How embedded are we in our stories and how well do they serve us? You be the judge.

Bill Chiu

- **Age:** Fifty-eight
- **Residence:** Chicago area (Evanston), Illinois
- **Work:** Physician; oncologist, and surgeon
- **Marital Status:** Married thirty-five years; wife Emily
- **Children:** Todd, age thirty-two; Jeannine, thirty; Mike, twenty-eight
- **Major fear about aging after fifty:** "How I'll move into doing more and more short-assignment disaster-assistance medicine overseas and still have time to practice medicine as well as make my speaking-engagement commitments."
- **Biggest daily struggle after fifty:** Finding the time to manage our assets. I don't like to have others do it, yet it creates a real time crunch for me.

Bill is a physician. He's tall and slender, and has a presence that clearly suggests he means business. One of his neighbors, male and seventy-five, recently asked Bill when he planned to retire. The question stopped him cold. It's not that Bill hasn't planned for the financial security to retire. "That's been in the bank quite a while, though I keep worrying and adding money to a 401K." It's not that he doesn't sometimes tire of the pressure of practicing medicine and dream of calmer days. On top of his private medical practice, Bill also lectures and is an expert in disaster-relief medicine. His partners cover the workload for him when he's called to some disaster.

Bill realized that what he most wanted was to not be a clone of his retired neighbor at seventy-five. He had no idea who he'd be if he weren't practicing medicine. He had just assumed some transition would take care of itself or he'd work on it when the time came.

The meaning, the words and images, that Bill has crafted into the predominant story about himself goes like this: "I'm a really busy guy. I like it that way. It plays to my strengths. A major builder of retirement communities reports that nearly six out of ten baby boomers are likely to move to new homes for retirement. The new home, maybe, but relocate? That's not for me. The kids are gone, though I still worry about them all the time. I think there's fate and we're controlled by it. My experience is pretty much the norm. Emily has plenty to keep her busy with her memberships and meetings and volunteer work. Someday I'll get some disease or have a stroke or a heart attack. I hope I'll die quickly. In the meantime, what rewards me is my ability to rationally and logically address problems and come up with smart solutions. Why would I ever give that up?"

We know that Bill's self-identified identity anchors are:

GREAT DOCTOR   WORLD TRAVELER
MEDICAL LECTURER   BUSY   INTENSE

Analysis:

- Of the three Truths (pages 3–5), which ones are important in Bill's situation?
- Of the ten Realities (page 52), which ones are important in Bill's situation?
- Analysis of Bill's identity ability: How will Bill's current identity anchors be helpful to him? How could they be a hindrance to him?
- Analysis of Bill's meaning-making ability: How will Bill's current stories about himself be helpful to him? How could they be a hindrance to him?
- Evidence of Bill's willingness to assume the corollary responsibilities.

Laura Ellison

- **Age:** Eighty-two
- **Residence:** Seattle, Washington
- **Work:** Psychiatric social worker, retired; still active with patient-advocacy work
- **Marital Status:** Widowed for forty years
- **Children:** Phyllis, age sixty, Mary, fifty-eight, Robert, fifty-five, Phillip, fifty-three, Thomas, forty-seven; thirteen grandchildren

"It's been a while since I was anywhere near fifty, but I well remember thinking I desperately needed an identity beyond mother and widow. I was afraid it would never happen. My husband had died leaving me with five children. By the time they were all showing signs of independence, it was time for me to go back to graduate school and make something of myself."

Biggest fear after fifty: Losing my faculties and becoming dependent on my children.

Biggest daily struggle after fifty: Running out of energy before I run out of things to do.

Laura looks like many people's image of a grandmother: silver hair, round face, kind eyes, glasses, ready smile, and gentle voice. Clothes were never a big thing for her and still aren't, though she likes unusual jewelry. Laura was widowed early. She and the children remained in the home she and her husband had bought together. A year after her husband died, Laura applied to graduate school. Her undergraduate degree was in nursing, and she still had her RN license, so a graduate program in nursing was an ideal choice. Although she knew no one when she began to apply, by the time she'd submitted her application she knew a great number of people very well, as was her usual style. Her application was rejected because she was viewed as "too old to have enough good working years left to make graduate school a good investment on Laura's part and her scholarship a good investment on the school's part." By her own admission, Laura went "nuts," threatening to make what she saw as their "sexist, ageist, elitist" response public in the media "I'm one of those people who thinks she is an individual first and responsible for her own destiny," she said. Quietly but persistently, Laura aligned herself with powerful people in the press and in other graduate-school groups. Then she took one prominent TV person and one from the press with her to a meeting she had arranged with the dean of the graduate school. Laura was admitted. This experience also moved her attention from patient care to patient advocacy, a discipline she helped pioneer after receiving her master's degree with honors. Laura never remarried. She immersed herself in her children, her work, her church, her passion for advocacy, and good works, with travel on special trips with friends added for good measure. Along the way she discovered photography, which has become almost as big a love for her as her family continues to be. Laura also remains very active in the church she has belonged to for decades.

The meaning, the words and images, that Laura has crafted into the predominant story about herself goes like this: "I've declared this the "Year of Laura" to all my family and friends. I suspect I'm running out of time. I fell at a meeting in a nearby hotel recently, and that was a real wake-up call. I've spent years giving my time and energy away. I've been happy to do it, but it's time I took a whole lot of time for myself. I have boxes of things I've been going to work on for years: delayed reading, scrapbook materials, images to create with my cameras, and local places to see that I've never visited. I mean to live alone until they carry me out of here. I'm not likely to take kindly to people fussing over me, no matter how well intended. I love my family, but I can see that slowly releasing them—and me—is a much kinder way to anticipate death than going like gangbusters and then falling over. I may look like everybody's grandmother, but I'm a tough lady, and people will have a hard time dissuading me or convincing me of a better approach now that I've made up my mind."

We know that Laura's self-identified identity anchors are:

MOTHER AND GRANDMOTHER   SECRETLY SLOWING DOWN A BIT
SOCIAL ACTIVIST   INDEPENDENT   RELIGIOUS

Analysis:

- Of the three Truths (pages 3–5), which ones are important in Laura's situation?
- Of the ten Realities (page 52), which ones are important in Laura's situation?
- Analysis of Laura's identity ability: How will Laura's current identity anchors be helpful to her? How could they be a hindrance to her?
- Analysis of Laura's meaning-making ability: How will Laura's current stories about herself be helpful to her? How could they be a hindrance to her?
- Evidence of Laura's willingness to assume the corollary responsibilities.

Not all relationships and communities should or will last a lifetime. Not all relationships will meet our needs forever.

Chapter 8

Community Ability:
What Do You Mean,
The Right Mix of Relationships?

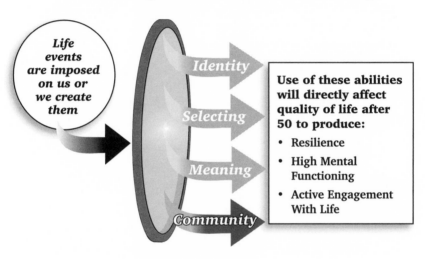

Most of us belong to a variety of communities, and have a set of relationships within them and separate from them. If we have younger children who are in school and are involved in scouts or sports, a significant number of our relationships derive from our frequent contact with other parents. Physical proximity accounts for some relationships; we rely on our neighbors to bring in our mail or feed the cat when we're on vacation. We also have institution- and affinity-related relationships: those centered around shared affiliation with employers; schools; club activities such as golf or gun collecting or antiquing; religious institutions; civic organizations; twelve-step programs; or neighborhood committees. Extended family relationships can play a big role in our sets of communities. Some relationships may last a lifetime; others may last a brief while before departing for a short time or forever.

We're free and able to choose the relationships and communities we belong to. We might not exercise that ability, and we might make poor choices sometimes, but the freedom and ability are there.

The awareness and exercise of community and relationship ability will be essential because it sets the social conditions—and the likelihood of lifelong learning and lifelong development —in which we'll live our lives during an extended period after fifty that's as yet uncharted for us, regardless of how much planning and anticipating we've done.

To better understand relationships and communities, it's important to understand social convoys, individual attributes, and relationship characteristics.

Social Convoys

We travel our life's road in the company of others. This company, a community, can be seen as a social convoy. Imagine a group of ships crossing an ocean together, separate yet somehow connected and interdependent. We require others for our own success and development, and we have relationships with people to celebrate the good times as well as to support us in the bad times. Some of us prefer smaller convoys and some prefer larger. Some of us change our preferences during our life spans. Most of us belong to multiple convoys simultaneously whether we're aware of it or not.

Within those social convoys we have relationships with individuals, including with ourselves. People join or leave our convoys periodically, many varying greatly in their length of convoy membership. Some will leave with advance notice or fanfare; others without warning or without making a sound.

It's time to use your notebook again. Take a few minutes to make a short list of the social convoys that you're a member of. What stands out for you about your convoys? What do you think might stand out for others about your convoys?

Individual Attributes

All the individuals we have relationships with have individual attributes, characteristics that are true of those people regardless of where they are or the situation they find themselves in. Some examples:

- gender
- education
- marital status
- height
- skill sets
- eye color
- biographical details

Individual attributes remain permanent, or at least stable, until we change them or add new ones. Then they become stable again as new or altered attributes (a college degree or gray hair or marital status, for example).

Phyllis Plubert, forty-nine, lives in Chicago. A mother of six, the youngest of whom is seventeen, Phyllis teaches sixth grade in one of Chicago's more "problematic" public schools. She and her husband, Jerry, also a college graduate, have lived in the same house for the past twenty years. Phyllis has a growing interest in sociology, political science, and human development. These individual attributes remain true of her whether she's in Chicago or Nome.

William Magunda, fifty-six, lives in Omaha, Nebraska, and owns a small chain of very successful restaurants. He didn't go to college, and he married later in life; he and his wife,

Clarisse, have no children. William is six feet, one inch tall. He's a very hard worker and likes being an entrepreneur. These individual attributes remain true of William whether he's in Omaha or Rome.

Take a few minutes to think about your individual attributes and list them in your notebook. What stands out for you about your individual attributes? What might stand out for others about your individual attributes?

Relationship Characteristics

The relationships we have also have characteristics separate from our individual attributes. Examples of relationship characteristics include:

- frequency of contact; how often do we connect?
- types of information exchanged; what do we talk or write about?
- shared experiences or friendships; what pieces of our biographies do we have in common?
- impact on sense of self and ways of operating; how does our relationship affect our sense of ourselves and how we move about in the world each day?
- emphasis on familiar or on unfamiliar; do we tend to emphasize what we already know in our relationship, or do we tend to emphasize what one or neither of us knows yet?
- activities, interests, or goals shared; which of these do we have in common that strengthen our relationship?
- level of trust; how much do we trust each other?
- impact on decision making; how does our relationship affect decisions either of us might be making?
- It's important to remember that these characteristics can be understood or measured from either person's view-

point, are subject to rapid change, and exist only so long as the people remain in relationship.

Phyllis Plubert has taught in the Midwest for many years. Her friendships with a lot of her students' parents lasted well beyond the kids' enrollment at her school. The characteristics of those relationships included a shared commitment to the children's development, the level of trust Phyllis and the parents had for each other, how often they connected, and the information they exchanged about the students' progress and what the parents could do at home to help. As the students graduated, some of the characteristics of those relationships were no longer true, and some of the relationships have dissolved entirely.

William Magunda built his professional life around his twelve restaurants. His relationships are primarily with the managers and his suppliers. Active in his state's restaurant association, he also has relationships with many other restaurant owners. The characteristics of those relationships include a shared love of managing restaurants, participation in teams solving customer-service and food-quality problems, a tendency to meet at professional conferences more than at social events, frequent contact related to problem solving, and a shared interest in emerging restaurant technologies.

What did you notice about the relationship characteristics for Phyllis and William?

Choose one of your relationships that's important to you. Take a few minutes to list the relationship characteristics for each of you in it. Now choose a second relationship that's important to you. Again, list the relationship characteristics for each of you. In each relationship, what surprises or informs you based on your relationship preferences? What surprises or informs you based on what you think are the other person's relationship preferences?

Fifty and Beyond—Individual Attributes And Relationship Characteristics

It's very common, in our personal and professional lives, to confuse individual attributes with relationship characteristics. This leads to all kinds of problems at home (in expectations, communication, negotiation, and satisfaction) and at work (in selection, hiring, performance, and promotion).

As we become fifty and beyond, using knowledge of convoy management, individual attributes, and relationship characteristics enables us to create and change the community memberships and the relationships we really need. Exercising our relationship and community ability is directly tied to skills and agility.

Accustomed as many of us are to personal independence as our gold standard in life, it's time to turn our attention to creating a balance between dependence and independence. The drive for independence served us well as a motivator for development and individuation earlier in life. Dependence, so long as it wasn't overdone, served us well as a social glue and a catalyst in developing trust and belonging.

As we move beyond fifty, absolute independence and absolute dependence will fade for most of us as freestanding conditions. We'll have a certain amount of independence in our lives. What that will look like, and how it will change and be managed, is an individual choice. We'll also have a certain amount of dependence (perhaps *reliance* is a better word—less baggage); what that will look like and how it will change and be managed is also an individual choice.

What will need to increase in importance is *interdependence,* a condition in which we can care for each other, requesting, offering, and exchanging value wisely and gracefully without tampering with the independence/dependence balance each of us creates for him- or herself every day. Working with interdependence is a characteristic and a skill that flows from community and relationship ability. Our capacity for inter-dependence can feature strongly in the success of our skills and agility.

> *In an interdependent situation, the golden eggs are the effec-tiveness, the wonderful synergy, the results created by open communication and positive interaction with others. And to get those eggs on a regular basis, we need to take care of the goose. We need to create and care for the relationships that make those results realities.*
>
> Stephen R. Covey, *The 7 Habits of Highly Effective People*

Our ability to create effective interdependence well beyond fifty will be directly linked to how well we exercise our relation-ship and community ability and the related responsibilities.

What's the minimum number of people required for commu-nity? Two. The maximum number of people possible in commu-nity? It depends on: (1) The relationship characteristics you've decided you need; (2) Your effectiveness in making it happen enough (*enough* is subject to personal interpretation); and (3) Your clarity about your own changing needs. How many com-munities are enough? It depends on how many communities you need to be a member of to have all the relationship char-acteristics you want in your life.

Research on aging confirms the importance of peer group in maintaining quality of life. The problem is, the older we get, the more the sizes of our convoys tend to shrink. People we've relied on, including our spouses, lose their health, move away, or give up interests and activities that used to bring us togeth-er. Convoys—communities or clusters of communities—have to be built and rebuilt as we go along at fifty and beyond.

Strong and Weak Relationships And Convoys

The central unit in every convoy is the relationships between two or more people, which tend to cluster as *strong convoys* and *weak convoys*. Strong and weak don't suggest superior or inferior; neither do they suggest morality, loyalty, or importance.

Strong Convoys are clusters of relationships characterized by so much shared experience, knowledge, opinion, culture, and history that, however long you've known each other, it feels like a long time. Strong convoys are efficient: there's a lot that needn't be spoken or explained; there are lots of relationships in common, and lots of opinions and ideas shared so strongly that discussion is unnecessary. We all need strong convoys to spend time with, turn to in times of trouble, and share our favorite activities and joys with. These are the people who will understand.

Weak Convoys are clusters of relationships characterized by little shared experience, knowledge, opinion, culture, or history. Many things have to be explained or discussed. There are few relationships in common. Weak convoys bring us new information, different ideas, fresh relationships, varying perspectives, and people we don't know who have knowledge we're unlikely to have.

We all need both kinds of convoys, and both strong and weak relationships as well. Creating relationships and convoys, and the management abilities that lead to skills and agility, all have to do with maintaining the appropriate (an individual decision) balance of strong and weak given our needs at any point.

For an example of the life—and demise—of a convoy, I've chosen a Jake Page story of the Crow Indians.

One erstwhile Crow warrior lived for four decades on the reservation in Montana but ended his autobiography with the end of the old-life ways. "Nothing happened after that," he wrote. "We just lived. There were no more war parties, no capturing of horses...no buffalo to hunt. There is nothing more to tell.

Without the hunt, much of the seasonal work of the tribes was gone—both men's and women's work. New ways of achieving status—or foregoing it—had to be devised. War leaders and the warrior societies and indeed most of the men's societies, lost their reasons for being and began to disappear.

Jake Page, *In The Hands of the Great Spirit*

The people's individual attributes remained the same or were changed and then re-stabilized. The relationship characteristics changed dramatically. The strong convoys dissipated with the devaluing of shared history, the evaporation of common purpose, and the sharing of information and action. The Crow were isolated on the reservation. Weak-convoy benefits—new knowledge, other options, different relationships, fresh possibilities—were available only if people left the reservation. It was impossible for those who stayed to seize weak-convoy opportunities.

Let's meet Janet Faulkner and Cliff Snider, and work with information on them to understand their relationships and convoys. Also, we'll look at how each of them can exercise relationship and community ability to develop the convoys and interdependent support that will support our own skills and agility well after fifty.

Janet Faulkner

- **Age:** Seventy-three
- **Residence:** Kansas City, Missouri
- **Work:** Catholic Sister, teaching order
- **Major fear about aging after fifty:** "Being exclusively with older women."
- **Major daily challenge after fifty:** "Keeping my spirits up when facing the negative media blitz about the geopolitical future of this planet and all of us. There are days I can't bear to watch any TV broadcasters. They aren't doing us any favors by playing so strongly to the sensational and frightening."

Sr. Janet Faulkner is a wiry, dark-haired woman with bright, brown eyes and considerable intuition. She's wearing a solid color skirt with a contrasting solid-color jacket and a print blouse that unites skirt and jacket visually. These triple combinations are the essence of her wardrobe. Wearing a small cross on a gold chain, she comes into the room with her eyes cast downward, sits, and puts her hands in her lap. Then she looks up at me and says, with a grin, "I've brought you a book to read. Start with the passage I marked. When you come to understand that passage, you'll understand a lot about me."

I took the book home and read it over several nights. It was *Some Do Care* by Anne Colby and William Damon. The marked passage said:

> *Of all the capacities that contribute to positivity in moral exemplars, the one most directly linked to their framework of values is the capacity to forgive. Forgiveness and mercy are widely recognized values in Western moral and religious traditions, and they were endorsed by practically all of our exemplars. Nevertheless, forgiveness and mercy are hard to sustain in the crucible of real life. Just like the rest of us,*

moral exemplars encounter persons who are difficult to for-
give. In fact, because of the nature of their work, moral ex-
emplars more than most are tested in their capacities for
charitable responding—a special irony, since charity is of-
ten high in their priority of moral values.

Janet was born seventy-three years ago in Buffalo, New York, the youngest of four children, the only girl. Two of her brothers are gone now. She was close to them throughout their lives, and remains close to her surviving brother. As a youngster Janet had a reputation for being a tomboy and "smart as a whip, which got me into lots of trouble if I couldn't stop myself from saying what was on my mind."

Throughout high school—she went to all Catholic schools—Janet was inspired by the nuns' dedication to the development of the young women in their charge, especially to teaching the ability to think. "I found myself believing in a universal being but also in my own need to be self-determined. Reconciling those two was a struggle for years. Janet found herself admiring the way the Sisters could challenge ideas, and was constantly amused, though she had to conceal it, by the number and variety of things they could hide for days in the pockets of those voluminous black skirts. By her junior year in high school Janet felt called. No one recruited her; in fact, none of the Sisters ever suggested it to her. Eventually, Janet went to her father, who was shocked, and together they went to her mother. Mrs. Faulkner wept; then, having cried herself out, never questioned her daughter's choice again. One month after graduating from high school, Janet entered the convent. She has loved her life as a Sister and has few regrets.

Previously known as Sister Mary Thomas, Janet spent the next forty-four years becoming the best Sister she could be. She taught school—first math and science, then adding Latin and composition. She taught in the Midwest—elementary school, then high school—for many years, punctuated by teaching in

India for five years, and retired six years ago. Sister Janet is just completing five years as a member of her province's governance board, and has the right to a sabbatical before choosing the next focus for her efforts.

My research asked for a list of up to fifteen people, still living, who have the greatest effect on the participant's sense of him- or herself and how he or she operates in the world each day. Thus we know that Janet's relationships and convoys look like the table on page 98.

We know that Janet's self-identified identity anchors are:

> SISTER   RETIRED   WELL-INTENTIONED
> SEARCHING   TENACIOUS

Analysis:

- Of the three Truths (pages 3–5), which ones are important in Janet's situation?

- Of the ten Realities (page 52), which ones are important in Janet's situation?

- Analysis of Janet's identity ability: How will Janet's current identity anchors be helpful to her? How could they be a hindrance to her?

- Analysis of Janet's meaning-making ability: How will Janet's current stories about herself be helpful to her? How could they be a hindrance to her?

- Evidence of Janet's willingness to assume the corollary responsibilities.

- Analysis of Janet's social convoys: How do you assess the quality and sufficiency of Janet's strong and weak convoys?

Cliff Snider

- **Age:** Seventy-three
- **Residence:** Omaha, Nebraska
- **Work:** Retired aeronautical engineer
- **Marital Status:** Single; wife, Helen, died five years ago
- **Children:** Jennifer, age fifty; Paul (deceased)
- **Major fear about aging after fifty:** "Being put so far out to pasture that I can't see the barn."

Major surprise about aging after fifty: "What it takes to date again at my age"
Major struggle after fifty: "Daily fear that I've failed to fulfill the promise of my life and that it's way too late for me to make up the difference now."

After college and his service in the US Air Force, Cliff worked for a major American aircraft corporation throughout his career. Planes and flying have been his life. Helen mostly raised the kids. Cliff's work required a lot of travel and a huge number of relationships with the military, vendors, research organizations, and in his own company. Cliff retired at sixty-five, "only because they made me." He joined the board of the local flight museum. He and Helen traveled the States. They loved their grandchildren. Three years into Cliff's retirement, Helen had a heart attack and died. A few months later their son, Paul, died in an auto accident. Cliff was always close to his daughter, Jennifer, and now he's even closer to her and her family.

Cliff has kept the house in much the same shape Helen left it in. He's considered selling it and moving to a condo, but that doesn't feel right yet. During the past three years he's gotten active in Omaha grassroots politics, become involved in the church again, taken some Senior Hostel trips, welcomed visits with his buddies from work—all now retired—as they drove through Nebraska in their RVs, and watched TV until he thought he would scream.

Name	Kind and length of relationship	How often contact?	Types of information shared	Impact on sense of self and ways of operating
Susan Thomas	Religious sister 45 years	daily	Order news Personal concerns Health Politics Travel Yoga	Very high
Ben Faulkner	Brother 73 years	weekly	Family History Health	High
Carol Green	Former student, long-time friend 37 years	3–4 times per week	News Books Politics	Very high
Bud Faulkner	Nephew	monthly	Family History Sports	Low
Carrie Brede	Rel. Sister	daily	Personal	Medium
Annie Phillips	Rel. Sister	weekly	Order news Politics Sports Yoga	High
Carrie Thomas	Rel. Sister	daily	Daily tasks Spiritual concerns	High
Tim Sullivan	Friend; Husband of Carol Green	biweekly	Humor News Politics	High

Emphasis on familiar	Activities shared	Level of trust	Impact on decision making
High Low	Yoga Order meetings Governance	Very high	High
High Low	None any more	Very high	Low
Low High	Meals Travel Shopping Whatever Tim Sullivan dreams up	Very high	High
High Low	Family dinners Baseball games	Low	Low
High Low	Television Tasks	Medium	Low
High Medium	Order business Movies Theater Retreats	High	Low
High Low	Yoga Shopping Movies Theater	High	High
Low High	Whatever Tim dreams up	Very high	High

After a lot of soul searching, Cliff has concluded that he needs to make some major changes. He thought of the Peace Corps or Vista but gave that up. He says, "The Lord helps those who help themselves. But he only helps them after a demonstration of follow-through and firepower on their part." What Cliff really wants is companionship. That means dating. "This is a world that converted from shirts and ties to sloppy jeans and ugly T-shirts while I wasn't looking. Surely I can't be the only one noticing certain kinds of changes no one warned me about. Hair, for instance. I've got less of it where it used to be and more of it in places I didn't used to have places. Sometimes I look in the mirror and see images of my parents' faces looking back at me. I have to smile. Aren't I the one who ran away from home, determined to be as different from them as possible? On top of that, if you had told me Rogaine and Viagra would be commonly used for dating-related purposes I'd have had you locked up. But it's true for lots of guys in my position."

Cliff is very able in many ways, a man of accomplishment and determination, and ready for the kinds of changes that are low in control and high in influence—not his style until now.

We know from the research that Cliff's relationships and convoys look like the table on page 102.

We know that Cliff's self-identified identity anchors are:

ENGINEER   MARRIED   AGING
LONELY   DIFFICULT

Analysis:

- Of the three Truths (pages 3–5), which ones are important in Cliff's situation?

- Of the ten Realities (page 52), which ones are important in Cliff's situation?

- Analysis of Cliff's identity ability: How will Cliff's current identity anchors be helpful to him? How could they be a hindrance to him?

- Analysis of Cliff's meaning-making ability: How will Cliff's current stories about himself be helpful to him? How could they be a hindrance to him?
- Evidence of Cliff's willingness to assume the corollary responsibilities.
- Analysis of Cliff's social convoys: How do you assess the quality and sufficiency of Cliff's strong and weak convoys?

Name	Kind and length of relationship	How often contact?	Types of information shared	Impact on sense of self and ways of operating in the world
Jennifer Conley	Daughter 48 years	Daily	Domestic Health Family	Very High
Mike Conley	Son in law 26 years	Weekly	Domestic Health Family	Medium
Trisha Conley	Granddaughter 22 years	Monthly	Family Trisha's life after college	Medium
Tim Conley	Grandson 19 years	Weekly	Sports Family Tim's athletics and community college activities	Medium
Bill Marstein	Former Coworker 23 years	Monthly	Update on old friends Sports Military History	Low
Nancy & Steve Wambaugh	Neighbors 8 years	Weekly	Neighborhood news	Low
Harry Kradock *(Republican Precinct Committee)*	Friend 3 years	Weekly	Local Politics	Medium
Paul Sims	Minister 2 years	Weekly	Domestic Health Family Church	Medium

Emphasis on familiar Emphasis on unfamiliar	Activities shared	Level of trust	Impact on decision making
High Low	Tim's athletic events	Very High	Medium
High Medium	Tim's athletic events	High	Low
Medium High	None	Very High	Low
High Low	Sports	Very High	Low
Medium Low	None	High	Low
High Low	None	Medium	Low
Low High	Precinct activities	Medium	Low
Medium Medium	Church services	High	Low

When we were young we made "yes or no" choices. Now we're free to select, more carefully and without undue fear, from a broader range of possibilities.

Chapter 9

Selecting Ability: Learning to Select Instead of Choose

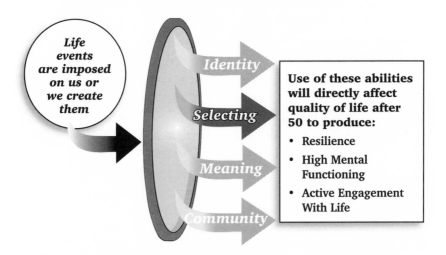

Decisions, decisions, decisions. When we were children we longed to be allowed to make them. Most children learn to make good decisions by practicing. Some of their decisions are excellent; some are poor, just like adults' decisions. What are the major features of most childhood decision making?

- They're usually binary: yes/no, okay/not okay.
- Permission is often required.
- Thinking about and making the decision involves acquiring experience.
- Usually, we have adults to fall back on.

- Deciding is part of the process of "growing up" and is used as evidence of our progress.
- We aren't necessarily good yet at distinguishing the best options to decide among.
- The decisions are usually smaller in comparison to later-in-life "adult decisions."

Earlier in our lives we made impulsive decisions. We sought our parents' advice or we didn't. We decided to belong or be different from. We made yes/no decisions about cars, husbands, houses, wives, and jobs in the various acquiring and jettisoning periods in our lives. We flipped coins. We made lists of pluses and minuses. We used brilliant logic or we looked to intuition. We listened to our emotions. Hope and fear drove our decisions. We asked our friends for advice. We ignored our elders. We ignored our friends. We listened to everyone other than ourselves. We listened only to ourselves. We had a lot of ways to arrive at decisions, effective and ineffective ways that produced good and bad decisions. How very human of us.

Barry Molden was sixteen when he bought his first car, a five-year-old Honda, with money he'd saved combined with money he'd talked his grandmother out of (his first real sales job). His parents were unenthusiastic about his decision, but elected not to outvote him on this one. Three weeks after he bought the car, he had an accident three blocks from his house; he was unhurt, but the car was badly damaged. His parents and grandmother said, "Oh, well, it was a very good lesson for Barry, and not an exceptionally expensive one. Next time he'll have learned."

Early in our lives, the two overriding decision factors (which, after fifty, take on the greater flavor of selection) were:

- The world gave us permission to be in a learning mode, which meant we were cut some slack if our decision process or outcome wasn't great.

- We had lots of recuperative years to recover from poor decisions or to create new directions.

After fifty, however, deciding often becomes selection, and the possibilities are seldom simply binary. The complexity of our decision making is usually due to changes in the world around us, the mushrooming of new possibilities and technologies that we hadn't considered before, the change in our identities, meaning-making, and communities, the shortened life span of a valid decision, and the array of dynamic tensions and competing priorities we face as change accelerates. Still, in the midst of all this, skills and agility are inevitably directly and indirectly associated with exercising our ability to select.

There's a secret to exercising our selection ability after fifty. Very few decisions get and stay made across our life spans. Most have to be remade—perhaps several times. For anyone with a strong preference for closure and having things permanently settled, this can be crazy-making. Twenty-seven years ago, Avery and Audie Blue decided to marry. That was the last permanent decision either can remember making in their full life together.

Making selections at fifty and much later isn't for sissies, particularly as we approach "elderly." We'll have to make selections about our financial management, healthcare (including forms of membership and insurance for ourselves and others), planning, identity, meaning-making, communities, and social and professional activities, to name a few. And we won't have as many years to recover from poor decisions as we had in our thirties.

Two years ago, Greg Oakley, fifty-seven, sold his business. He wanted to retire. Then each of his competitors, one of whom had bought Greg's company, started courting him to do consulting work for them on his terms. He hadn't dreamed this possibility existed as he slowly rediscovered his love of his expertise. Now he's working four days a week, and likes it even better than his developing interest in growing grapes and making wine—all the fun and little of the responsibility.

So what's different about selection ability at fifty and beyond? My research disclosed five dominant factors in decisions that research participants had made or were facing:

1. Many decisions refuse to stay made. Something changes, and what we thought was a permanent decision becomes part of a series of selections.

2. Thinking about and making the selection still involves acquiring new information as well as relying on previous information and experience. The possibilities are often embedded in dynamic tensions.

3. Not deciding is a valid form of decision making, but only for a while.

4. Great deciding is much less frequently "yes or no" than it is a process done with: a. dynamic tensions in mind; b. the polar forces at work in most significant adult decisions; and c. making selections from a field of possibilities.

5. Increasingly, the best selections are made with the needs of our significant others in mind as well as our own. Joint selections will become more common as interdependence replaces the extremes of independence and dependence.

Real maturity is always meeting what's in front of you in this way. Although true maturity may be rare, we are all capable of it and can recognize it when we see it. When our lives are touched by a mature person we feel it.

Norman Fischer, *Taking Our Places*

The world, and we ourselves, have very different expectations and tolerances regarding selection ability beyond fifty. Remember how much slack we were willing to cut young people as we gave them permission to learn? After fifty we're not usually given so much slack in people's expectations of us or our expectations of ourselves. And life is far too complex and changes too fast for most of us to capture everything we need with a traditional plus-and-minus sheet or a yes/no approach.

Here are two secrets to exercising selection ability at fifty and beyond:

Understand that all major decisions are actually composites, assessing what our individual or shared comfort zone is between one or more sets of dynamic tensions. To understand selection we must pay attention to dynamic tensions, the equally true opposites that frame our selection process.

Examples: (1) On one hand, our beloved grandchildren live down the street; on the other, the weather's much nicer far away. (2) On one hand, there's nothing wrong with our car; on the other, we can well afford a better one, and one of us gets great pleasure from cars. (3) On one hand, most of our colleagues have retired and taken their familiar companionship with them; on the other, struggling through just one more year of full-time work will make a difference in our annual income. (4) On one hand, one member of a couple has retired and is ready to move on; on the other, the other half of the couple is really enjoying and stimulated by his or her work. (5) On one hand, we're comfortable where we are; on the other, so many of our dreams are waiting for us to fulfill them, and we're much less likely to succeed if we operate only from where — in time, place, mindset, situation — we are now.

We face all kinds of decisions that, once made, won't stay made. We make investments that were good when we made them and got less good later. We sell the house because the kids are gone, and then discover, despite all our research and soul-searching, that we don't really like living in an "adult community." We decide to retire, having had enough of the world of jobs, and then discover what only direct experience can confirm: we really need and want to work part-time. We decide to move near our children, whereupon they get transferred and move. (Author's confession: I once made an investment decision based on proximity to my granddaughters in the San Francisco Bay area. Within weeks, my son accepted a job in Singapore, and they all promptly moved there.) We decide to change doctors so we'll have a younger or more highly recommended one, and she promptly moves to a different health-care system. Some decisions stay made across our life spans; we have to remake others several times.

Remember the secrets to exercising selection ability at fifty and beyond: Assume that many decisions are incremental, subject to monitoring, updating, and changing. This will help you set realistic expectations and save you a lot of grief, especially if you have a strong preference for getting things settled and wanting them to stay put.

Mary Murray, sixty, was an executive assistant at a global travel company. Her boss was retiring, and Mary didn't want to go through the agony of breaking in—and being broken in by—yet another senior officer, so she decided to take retirement too. For the first six weeks she had a great time, then it began to bother her that most of her friends were still working full-time, as was her husband. Her grandchildren were in school each weekday. She wasn't as inspired as she'd expected to be by the volunteer organizations she explored. Mary tried to go back to work at the tour company, only to discover that many of America's tax and employment laws are neither retirement-friendly nor work-friendly.

What was a talented woman to do? This wasn't just a bad case of deciding on Mary's part. She did a fair amount of research with others who'd made this choice. She had planned and thought it through. What she hadn't yet done was have the actual experience. Sometimes, external or unforeseen circumstances cause a decision to unmake itself. In this case, Mary was never really going to know until she tried it.

Take a few minutes to write, in your notebook, your last five decisions, at least two of which must be significant ones. What was your starting place for each? Did you start in the appropriate place for each? What would you do differently if faced with the same situations again?

These selecting abilities are self-validating for people who are good at them. They prolong feelings of competence, insight, independence, identity, skillful creation and management of story, and management of relationships and convoys. Also, they require attentiveness and energetic effort.

Not deciding is a form of decision making. It sounds like a T-shirt slogan:

NOT TO DECIDE IS TO DECIDE!

The slogan could be interpreted in a derisive way and turned into a war of wills. One party in a relationship might continually drive for decision/closure ,while the other is continually pushing to keep options open in case new and better possibilities arise at the last minute.

The slogan could also be interpreted in a more Zen-like way: Deciding ability is ours. Decide or don't decide. Either way we decide.

Since we're bombarded by this vast shower every moment of our lives, we must expend a good deal of mental energy making sense of it all. We do so by first discarding most of the data that comes into our brains, and then categorize and simplify the actual information into neat packets of awareness and response—bytes of consciousness, as it were.

The result of this mental organizing effort is that our universe becomes scaled down to the level of our own capability to understand and process it.

— Harry R. Moody and David Carroll,
The Five Stages of the Soul

The skills-and agility-developing opportunity for all of us at fifty and beyond is to find the time and energy to stay conscious of what we're doing and what's happening around us. Exercising our selection ability includes the responsibility to pay attention!

Jim Morris, fifty-five, hates going to the dentist. There's a pattern to Jim's selections: Either he totally trusts the professional he's dealing with, and feels no need to understand the technical aspects of the expert's specialty; or he makes meaning, which in Jim's case includes believing that the professional is somehow doing shoddy work, or overcharging him for work Jim is unqualified to understand. This applies equally to dentists and auto-repair shops. Jim is a very busy man. His wife kept after him for months to make a dental appointment. When he finally went, he found he had serious gum problems, which would have been minor had he gone sooner. Did Jim decide or not? How effective was he at exercising the selection ability and taking on the corollary responsibilities? You be the judge.

Great deciding is much less often "yes or no" than a process accomplished with dynamic tensions in mind, the competing factors at work in most significant decisions. For example, would you rather endure the annoyance of going to the dentist for a periodic checkup, or later endure the huge discomfort and cost of major gum surgery?

"Effective" selection doesn't mean making the "right" choice every time. A key to exercising our selecting ability well is understanding those underlying dynamic tensions that influence all the decisions we'll have to make and change. If we can help it, elderly is *not* the time to start developing an ability to work with these tensions.

Olivia and Henry Erickson, both seventy-one and retired, are deciding whether to buy a new car or put a chunk of money into their six-year-old Lexus. On its face it's a buy/no-buy decision, because if they don't buy a new car, they'll have to invest in their present one; keeping the cash isn't an option. In truth, the decision will actually be a composite of assessing their preferences or comfort zones on several dynamic tensions.

The Ericksons' tensions around deciding about the car:

- Henry's lifelong ambivalence about cars / Olivia's lifelong love affair with cars;
- Henry's preference for flying trips / Olivia's love of driving trips;
- Committing to a car payment for three years / Anxiety about surprise expenses arising;
- Henry wanting Olivia to have what she wants / Olivia wanting Henry to have what he wants.

By defining the most significant dynamic tensions together, Olivia and Henry's decision is much more likely to be clear, discuss-able, monitor-able, revisit-able, and livable.

The Ericksons have the money. They have selection ability. If they make the decision exclusively about the car, ignoring the dynamic tensions, they'll have missed an opportunity to work and communicate as people who are developing the skills and agility they need now and will need even more as their lives unfold toward "elderly."

I don't believe that we get more conservative and avoid taking risks in the second half, but experience does lead us to estimate the odds a little more closely. We begin to rely more on the advice of others, personal experience, available information, and a greater understanding of our own needs before we make shifts in our life portfolio. So if adults appear to take longer to make up their minds, well, it's true, because for most major decisions they have a bigger inventory of experiences to review.

James E. Birren and Linda Feldman, *Where to Go from Here*

Carol Diaz

- **Age:** Fifty-nine
- **Residence:** Los Angeles, California
- **Work:** SVP and regional director, regional banking system of a major national bank
- **Marital Status:** Partner of seventeen years, Stephanie Englund
- **Children:** None
- **Major fear about aging after fifty:** "Losing my energy."
- **Major surprise about aging after fifty:** "Not losing my energy."
- **Major daily struggle after fifty:** "I'm deeply afraid of becoming mediocre. One of the reasons I still work so hard at my job is that I know there's no possibility I'll ever be mediocre at work. In the rest of my life and future I'm not so convinced."

I go to Carol's office for our interview; she hasn't time to come to mine. I arrive at a plush banking floor high above Century City and am immediately ushered into an office that says, "I'm smart, successful, and don't need to brag about it. I've come a long way, baby." Carol's assistant offers me coffee, water, tea, or soda. Carol, just getting out of a meeting, sits down as if sitting at home, and asks with a bright smile, "Okay, where do we start? I'm finding this all interesting, so let's get on with it." Here is a woman who's ready and willing to more deeply understand her life and her development right now.

Carol came from a family with little money. Bright and female, not often the best of combinations in her youth, she was always industrious. From an early age she took all the jobs she could get, and all the education, too. Painful though it sometimes was for her parents that she was and wanted to be so different from what they were, they nevertheless consistently supported Carol's intentions and efforts. She worked in a local market. She won scholarships. For her career, she chose an industry that was big enough to offer significant opportunity, and was under enough legislative scrutiny to emphasize promoting capable women. She's proud of her achievements and of her family.

Carol and her longtime "gal," Stephanie, sixty-three, live in Santa Monica. Neither has children. Carol loves the life she leads and feels no need to change it yet. Stephanie, a real estate law attorney, has begun to long for a quieter life with less pressure, at least part of the time. The Coachella Valley, with its inviting desert towns, arises in conversation more and more often. Carol and Stephanie's is a very solid relationship, and the growing gap in their preferences is not a deal breaker. Nonetheless, they're both a bit anxious about how to navigate the decisions and conversations they've seen gradually approaching them.

Money will become a stretch only if they keep their home in Santa Monica *and* buy the expensive house they found in La Quinta. Stephanie worries about the drive back and forth on I-10. The traffic is awful and getting worse. They could telecommute some, but Carol really needs to work directly with her clients and staff most of the time.

Carol and Stephanie have decided that the most important choice facing them isn't whether to buy the house in La Quinta; it's the decision about Stephanie's retirement, which to Stephanie looks like going from full-time-plus to two days' work per week.

We know that Carol's self-identified identity anchors are:

PROFESSIONAL   PIONEER FOR PROFESSIONAL WOMEN
SUCCESSFUL   CORPORATE LEADER   DETERMINED

And we know that Carol's dynamic tensions look like this:

- Feeling career-completed/Not yet feeling career-completed
- Desire for sameness and stability/Desire for change and tolerance for risk
- Shared needs/Differing needs
- What's good for Stephanie/What's good for Stephanie and Carol

Analysis:

- Of the three Truths (pages 3–5), which ones are important in Carol's situation?
- Of the ten Realities (page 52), which ones are important in Carol's situation?
- Analysis of Carol's identity ability: How will Carol's current identity anchors be helpful to her? How could they be a hindrance to her?
- Analysis of Carol's meaning-making ability: How will Carol's current stories about herself be helpful to her? How could they be a hindrance to her?
- Evidence of Carol's willingness to assume the corollary responsibilities.
- Analysis of Carol's understanding of the selections she's facing?

Stuart Weintraub, Ph.D.

- **Age:** Sixty-six
- **Residence:** Denver, Colorado
- **Work:** CEO, high-tech medical specialties
- **Marital Status:** Married, forty-one years; wife Dorothy

- **Children:** Charlene, age thirty-six; William, thirty; six grandchildren

- **Major fear about aging after fifty:** "Something will happen to my wife, children, or grandchildren before it happens to me."

- **Major daily struggle after fifty:** "I lose words occasionally: people's names that I know perfectly well, names of things and places. It doesn't happen often, but often enough to really annoy me. I've done enough research to know this is common for men my age. Still, I'd rather it didn't happen."

Stuart grew up in a very stable family in Brooklyn. He retains his Brooklyn accent, though it has softened over the years. He uses his hands and face when he speaks, moving them rapidly in all directions. In his office, we're sitting in what he jokingly calls "Command Central," a room with several computers, monitors, a stack of banker boxes along one wall, pictures of his family on the desk, framed degrees on the walls, and a very unhealthy ficus tree in one corner. The office is set up so there's a circular path around the desk, giving Stuart access—often by rolling his chair, with him in it—to whatever he needs.

"I like your project," he says. "I haven't found enough people organizing great ways to organize and think and then leading us to do the work without giving us oversimplified answers or magical steps. On the other hand, participating in your research has opened up a whole lot of conversation between Dorothy and me. We're still at the figuring-out-the-key-questions stage. Later we'll move to answers."

Stuart is a well-educated man. He likes excellent colleagues and worthy opponents. He's famous for being impatient with people he thinks occupy the middle ground. His parents challenged his mind from the time he was born. His father, Max, didn't go to college. His mother, Betty, who worked with his father in the business, had gone to college and was perceived, when they wed, to be "marrying below her." Stuart has two younger brothers, both lawyers.

"My grandmother was sick a lot. Because she was a widow, and my mother was her only daughter, she lived with us most of the time I was growing up. I realize now that she had lost her role and way of living when my grandfather died. I can still smell her medicines and her room if I put my mind to it. It made me very curious about how people could get well and stay that way. Originally, I wanted to be a physician. When I was in high school I realized I just didn't like people enough to spend the rest of my life seeing them one at a time, day in and day out. I always liked science, mostly chemistry and physics. That started me down the path to medicine, high technology, and data management. I've done okay. Mom and Dad would be proud. I don't think I'm very different from most people. We're all in much the same boat, and life decides for us even if we think it doesn't."

"What's really up for Dorothy and me—and doing your research has driven it to the surface—is that we're in a paradoxical dilemma. We have all the assets, friends, stimulation, family, and opportunity we'll ever need. What we don't have—and we're both developing a hunger for it, with Dorothy in the lead—is simplification and what she keeps calling spaciousness, less of everything without surrendering our quality of life. I don't plan ever to retire; they'll have to carry me out. But still, we know we need to simplify and create spaciousness, two things I didn't set out to do and don't think I'm good at yet. Take a look at this clipping about George Steinbrenner."

> *George Steinbrenner has a retirement plan. It will permanently end his tumultuous, thrilling career in baseball. "You don't want to leave because you're a competitive human being and the juices are still flowing," Steinbrenner, the Yankees' principal owner, said. "So you just hope that you'll go out one day—horizontal." Steinbrenner extended*

his right hand and motioned to emphasize the position, nod-
ding as if to acknowledge the inevitable. Then a whisper:
"Yep, hor-i-zon-tal." This July 4, the man who once may
have thought he was invincible comes to his 74th birthday.
He now notices intimations of mortality.

The New York Times, May 2, 2004

"Pretty close to how I feel," Stuart says. "At the heart of everything is deciding. The universe takes over from there and pushes you to where you need to be." Then, not realizing that we were already deep into the interview, he slaps his desk hard and says, "Let's get to work. I don't have all day. When do we start?" We know that Stuart's self-identified identity anchors are:

SMART   INDEPENDENT   DRIVER
BUSINESS LEADER   FAMILY MAN

And we know that Stuart's dynamic tensions look like this:

- Allure of unknown simplification/Complexity feels like a comfort zone
- Dorothy's pushing/Stuart's resistance to pushing from any source
- No real need to change/Unidentified need to change

Analysis:

- Of the three Truths (pages 9–11), which ones are important in Stuart's situation?
- Of the ten Realities (page 52), which ones are important in Stuart's situation?
- Analysis of Stuart's identity ability: How will Stuart's current identity anchors be helpful to him? How could they be a hindrance to him?

- Analysis of Stuart's meaning-making ability: How will Stuart's current stories about himself help him? How could they be a hindrance to him?

- Evidence of Stuart's willingness to assume the corollary responsibilities.

- Analysis of Stuart's understanding of the selections he's facing?

The road will unfold each day within and outside of plan. Quality of life each day after fifty is directly linked to developing the necessary skills and agility.

Chapter 10

It's Called Your Life
For a Reason

I wrote this chapter to demonstrate the possibility that small but important changes to identity, meaning-making, relationships and communities, and selection can move us a long way after fifty. Avoiding the need for immediate closure will be important, as will avoiding the need to make large, dramatic changes in an attempt to hurry the process or minimize the anxiety that can accompany any change.

The number of us pioneering our after-fifty lives is unprecedented. No matter what, you're not alone as your road unfolds in the coming years.

Here's my point: usually all we get is a glimmer. A story we read or someone we briefly met. A curiosity. A meek voice inside, whispering. It's up to us to hammer out the rest. The rewards of pursuing it are only for those who are willing to listen attentively, only for those people who really care. It's not for everyone... These are the turning points from which we get to construct our own story, if we choose to so. It won't be easy and it won't be quick... It can be an endless process of discovery, one to be appreciated and respected for its difficulty.

Po Bronson, *What Should I Do With My Life?*

Life after fifty will require some healthy reinvention because practicing and developing our after-fifty skills and agility gives us more clarity and options.

We'll need to be skillful and agile with our losses and our achievements

Zach Mitsukoshi, sixty-nine, lost his wife and won a major architectural award in the same week. Mitzi had been a cancer patient for several years. She inspired everyone around her with her courage and will to live. After forty-seven years of marriage, Zach could read her face like a precious manuscript. He knew when she finally didn't want to fight anymore. He stayed with her as she slipped away. He'd lost not only his precious wife, but a forty-seven-year identity anchor: husband. Mitzi had pushed Zach to compete for the design work of the new library at the university. Despite grumbling that he was too old and slow, he threw himself into creating the design and won the competition; the impressive library had recently been completed. Today he'd returned there to be awarded a prize for design before a huge gathering. Mitzi had wanted this for him. Only as he stood there, award in his hand, did Zach truly realize how skillful and agile she had become, even in her illness.

We'll need to be skillful and agile in our roles and personal lives as many of the roles disappear

Author's note: I was a single parent for many years. "Pioneering male single parent" was a cornerstone among my identity anchors from the time my sons were young. They're now in their thirties and living on their own. Even given how satisfying I found the role, how appropriate an identity anchor is pioneering single parent for me today? I decided to retire this anchor to a shelf where I can appreciate its gifts to me, as well as what it took to earn it. I don't have to throw it away, though it's not a central identity anchor in my life after fifty. Some reinvention is healthy and appropriate here.

We'll need to be skillful and agile when we know we want change but don't yet know what it looks like

Sally Green, sixty-three, is a very good nurse. Sally thought she'd never consider slowing down from the combined commitments of hospital employment, her marriage, her grandchildren, church work, and volunteering. She loved the sense of competence and achievement it all gave her. This is how she'd lived her life for as long as she could remember. One night she awoke to the realization that she couldn't remember the last time she'd taken time for herself.

Not giving herself time used to be a source of pride; suddenly, it no longer seemed right. Did Sally need to reinvent herself or begin again? No. Had she made a mistake living her life almost exclusively for others? Absolutely not. Sally was confronting one of those after-fifty glimmerings requiring neither reinvention nor renovation. A small addition will be important, along with creating the space for it. What's necessary for Sally is knowing that she'll need additional skills and agility to move through her sixties and beyond with the grace she associates with herself.

Sally asked her husband and her best friend, Linda, to support and join her in her quest, and has pledged herself to practicing and developing the after-fifty skills and agility she'll need for the rest of her life. She embraces the idea of being her own skillful pioneer after fifty, and intends to be great at living after fifty, both inside and outside of plan each day.

We'll need to be skillful and agile around our changing world of work

According to Del Webb's annual Baby Boomer report, only 13% of survey respondents ages 44–56 said they won't work once their careers are over. Of the remainder, 43% said they definitely would work. Projecting, by 2015 the number of people between sixty and seventy-nine is expected to be 77 million. The worlds of work and of home environment are exploding with change, accelerated by the possibilities new technologies make possible.

Chloe Sonnenfeld, fifty-nine, has worked for several employers as a director and then vice president of human resources. Her children are long since out on their own. Chloe is smart enough to understand that she has primarily lived a life in which *doing* ("It didn't matter what—I just couldn't sit down for long.") will need to be matched by *being* for her to develop and sustain the after-fifty health she envisions for herself. Her husband, Keith, retired two years ago and has fallen in love with golf. Chloe has a huge range of interests, from astrology, to learning Spanish, to understanding her grandchildren as citizens of their own era. She loves her coworkers and many of her clients. She is, however, "tired of sweeping up after senior leaders who repeatedly fail to call me until a situation is well ablaze."

Chloe also understands the growing 24–7 work mindset that the leaders of her company are pushing, a mindset that's not a great fit for her. Chloe recently shocked a leader at her company by suggesting that the slogan he was promulgating ("Sleep is for the weak") wasn't good for the company and could eventually get him into trouble well beyond the time she could intervene and rescue him. Chloe's personal retirement assessment is:

- She's not ready to retire if retiring means not working at all.

- She won't be able to stay in her current job more than another year.

- She's never going to be someone who knits and cooks, though she considers several such people her dear friends.

- She has one more great job in her, preferably one that uses her current skill set but doesn't confine her to current skills or roles.

- She wants flexible part-time employment.

Chloe has begun working privately with a career coach while she continues working full-time at her job. A career coach at fifty-nine? Absolutely! Chloe is clear that career no longer means climbing the ladder. For her, it means finding the mutual right fit for another five years or more. This means using the professional services of someone with the career-search expertise Chloe didn't develop while she was building performance and survival skills with major employers.

In the process of doing this career work, Chloe has discovered to her chagrin that she's tied herself to some identity anchors that no longer serve her, has embedded herself in stories of being "stuck" in her current work (stories she and many of her coworkers tell each other regularly), needs to develop additional relationships and communities that can be great connections for her during and after her career transition, and has to make some clear selections after studying the dynamics involved and reviewing them with her husband. It all sounds like work to her, but no more work than staying where she is indefinitely. It won't be easy or quick; it can be an endless process of discovery, one to be appreciated and respected for its learning and development opportunities as well as its outcomes.

Chloe has decided to be smart and active in pioneering her own life after fifty. She's convinced that no one else will or should take more responsibility for her life than she should. There's a way for her to bring the best of her previous professional skills with her *and* develop the skills and agility she'll need after fifty.

> *In an ideal world, flexible retirement would allow employees to move in and out of the workplace seamlessly, without ever choosing a moment to retire... but in the United States, at least, things don't work that way for most employees of publicly held corporations... The obstacles start with pension and benefits regulations...."*

Ken Dychtwald, Tamara Erickson, and Bob Morison, "It's Time to Retire Retirement." *Harvard Business Review.*

We'll need to be skillful and agile in our planning

Mapping is no longer a great metaphor for a plan. In our era, the terrain as we pass fifty will be increasingly changeable and less map-able. The supplies and skills required along the way will change, sometimes multiple times, often in mid-journey. The destination might change dramatically or cease to exist long before we get there.

Jeb Hale, fifty-six, is a highly experienced draftsman, able with paper and pencil and all the software required for architectural drawings today. Twelve years ago, on his forty-fourth birthday, he went to work for a great architectural firm and has loved almost every day of his work life ever since. Divorced for eight years, Jeb has stayed connected to his children. He did solid financial planning for his future. Jeb's form of conscious career planning, which he took very seriously, looked much more like increasing skill and technical knowledge than like climbing the ladder. Work and kids and financial planning were his life.

Now, with both of his children away at college, Jed has met Barbara McGill, who's awakened ideas of remarriage and creating a shared life of greater balance. Also, it's rumored that Jeb's architectural firm is likely to be acquired by another firm, and the majority of its employees will be offered separation packages and encouraged to leave. As good as his performance is, Jeb thinks this will be his situation. He's tempted to be really angry about the potential change in his work life—this wasn't in the plan. But think about where Jeb might be if he'd had no financial or other plans at all.

> *It is important to distinguish between a real new beginning in someone's life and a simple defensive reaction to an ending. Each may exert a strain on a relationship, but the new beginning must be honored. The defensive reaction is simply a new way of perpetuating the old situation and needs to be considered as such.*
>
> William Bridges, *Transitions: Making Sense of Life's Changes*

All of this makes intelligent, reasonable-range planning and monitoring even more important than it would otherwise be. Planning is imperative, and can't be simply an extrapolation of the past into the future. We are the pioneers, and the pioneering work we have to do includes planning.

We'll need to be skillful and agile when what defined us before no longer works for us

Sam Coulette is a general partner in a large accounting firm. He rose through the ranks, always balancing his marketing efforts, which he excelled at but didn't particularly like, with his analytical and tax skills and billable hours. For a long time it was the perfect life. Sam and his wife, Lu, could afford a fine house in a great neighborhood. Their kids grew up there, never having to move. Sam loved his big car and his other toys, and he was recognized in his town as a civic leader. He enjoyed his partners, but particularly enjoyed his customers and the complexities of their businesses. Sam loved the challenges of living in several venues at once: home, office, client companies, and volunteer venues, and usually succeeding in all of them at once. He isn't sure what changed. He's sure that the demands of being so active and involved for so long turned from being a pleasure to feeling like a burden. Now fifty-nine, Sam would like a more private life with a bit less pressure. People aren't used to seeing him this way; he isn't used to it himself. After long talks with Lu, he's had to admit that he seems to be moving toward a different, as yet undefined, set of rewards. Many of the trappings of his success and proofs of achievement, while still great, just don't feed him anymore. He doesn't know what this means, but he's sure it won't be just about what he'll do next. It will have more to do with who he wants to be and how he wants to be each day. This isn't how Sam is used to crafting his life, and it has left him a bit scared.

We'll need to be skillful and agile in choosing our communities and how they define us

Penny Morris has been recovering from her accident for a year, which means adapting to using a wheelchair for the rest of her life. Penny had always been a great skier. For Penny's fifty-fifth birthday, she and her husband, Ron, went skiing. On a fast downhill run, someone collided with Penny. The impact paralyzed her from the waist down. She's done a lot of grieving. Penny can't do some of the things she used to do with their children and with her friends, but that's not what bothers her most. What really upsets her is that people treat her like she's disabled. She grasps the importance of understanding disabilities and the variety of community services and support available for disabled people. What her friends haven't come to grips with is that Penny is unwilling to use her dependence on a wheelchair as a condition of creating and belonging to community. She understands that she's not in the majority, and understands the wealth of belonging that could be hers. Still, she's decided that disability isn't going to be an identity anchor for membership in community. Her counselor has encouraged her to make conscious (and incremental) choices about this, knowing there's no necessity for a perfect or permanent choice. Ron will support her in whatever she decides.

We'll need to be skillful and agile in defining reasonable risks and what we really want

Rick was fired. Never mind that he'd been with the firm for twenty-four years; that he and the firm had grown up together; that he was one of its top three officers. The facts were: (1) It was a family-owned firm; (2) The founder had hired Rick twenty-four years ago; (3) The founder had recently died; (4) The company president (the founder's son) refused to hear "no" from Rick; and (5) Rick wasn't family. (6) Rick was fifty-one years old, a lifelong employee, whose identity and professional and social needs were totally tied up in his work and the company.

It took Rick a full year to find his footing. His friends kept checking in with him but he wasn't really available. When the dust settled, Rick saw himself as a fifty-two-year-old man with marketable CFO skills and the world to choose from. It wasn't easy to get there, but he faithfully did the work of arriving at possibilities. His wife, Ann, was open to big changes; now, so was he. They've just sold their Los Angeles home and have selected a mid-Atlantic town that they've fallen in love with. This means leaving their nearly grown children behind. It means networking and finding the right job, leaving their thirty-year communities behind, being able to afford to build the house they want in an area so much less expensive than LA, and taking the risks while they still see themselves as having recuperative years. Are they making the right choice? We won't know for years. Are they clear about what they want and how they want to be in the world each day? Absolutely.

Life after fifty can be a skillful and agile time for a lot of shared celebration

Congratulations. You are consciously face to face with the greatest opportunity so far. Given skill and agility, some of your most inspiring development and greatest contributions might well happen past fifty. The opportunity is yours. Your greatest tools can be lifelong learning and lifelong development. If you feel as though you need a refresher from time to time, go back to chapter 2 and apply its lessons to your life. We're not all willing to do the work of lifelong learning and lifelong development every hour of every day. Can we be informed and skillful enough to do the work regularly and consistently throughout the time we have left to us? I vote yes.

Finally

I wrote this book in hopes that we'll begin to create the greater vocabulary and the skills and flexibility we'll need as we progress from fifty to sixty, seventy, eighty, ninety, and beyond. So many more of us than ever before are going to be moving down this unfolding road. So many more of us are going to be personally responsible for the quality of our extended lives. So many more of us have an opportunity *now* to begin to develop the skills and agility we'll need for the rest of our lives in this fast-changing world. I wish you all resilience, high mental functioning, and active engagement with life for as long as your road unfolds.

Thanks for making this journey with me, taking the time to understand for yourselves, and to work with what I've offered. At the beginning of this book, I invited you to join me in a continuing conversation about life after fifty. I now repeat that invitation.

What looks to some readers like the end of this book looks like a beginning for others. The sign may say END but those of us practicing and developing our after-fifty skills and agility know that the sign is really about the end of our earlier limitations, not the end of our possibilities. The unfolding road lies before us and we are not alone.

> *"Beware the final solution: There is none."*
> –Betty Friedan, *The Fountain of Age*

About the Author

George H. Schofield, Ph.D., is an expert in lifelong human and organizational development, professional career management, and the art of balancing having an intelligent plan for ourselves with having the right skills and agility when life doesn't go according to plan. These abilities didn't materialize overnight. George's constants have been showing up, paying attention, and doing the necessary learning (not always perfectly).

His professional résumé includes VP/banker of a major international bank; regional director of services for a global career-transition and organizational consulting organization; founding principal of The Clarity Group in San Francisco; and strawberry picker in the Pacific Northwest. George's personal and volunteer lives include being a longtime single parent for his two sons; president of an advisory council on aging and disability services; baby rocker in a neonatal intensive care unit; and advisory-council member for a university undergraduate and graduate business school. His academic life includes an undergraduate degree in Business, two MA degrees focusing on Adult Learning/Development and Counseling, and a Ph.D. in Human and Organizational Development.

George and his wife, Linda de Mello, are longtime residents of the San Francisco Bay area.

The research he completed for this book came from George's need to understand what was really happening in the after-fifty lives of his friends, colleagues, and clients, as well as in his own life. As a professional researcher, author, speaker, and consultant, he had the basic tools, yet he knew we are only beginning to develop the language, insight, and content we'll need to successfully pioneer our after-fifty/before elderly lives. George hopes the book will be of value to you in your life for a long time to come.